S.99

'r   ho

On the Verge:
the Gypsies of England

by Donald Kenrick and Sian Bakewell

D1337596

Univers

First published by Runnymede Trust 1990

Second edition published 1995 in
Great Britain by
University of Hertfordshire Press
Library and Media Services
University of Hertfordshire
College Lane Hatfield
Hertfordshire AL10 9AB

ISBN 0-900458-57-7

Designed by
Beverley Stirling

Cover design and
page layout by
Kate Douglas

Cover photograph by
David Gallant

Printed by Watkiss Studios Limited

Contents

List of tables

Glossary

Gorgio A non-Gypsy.

Gypsy An abbreviation of the word 'Egyptian', a name given to the Romany people in the Middle Ages as it was thought they came from Egypt. The word is not in itself derogatory and we use it throughout as the general term. However in references to the 1968 Caravan Sites Act and subsequent policy, the meaning is that given in the Act, anyone of nomadic habit of life.

Romany As a noun: a member of a generally nomadic people originating in North India, the Romanies. An adjective relating to the culture, customs and language of the Romanies.

'Romany' From the word 'Rom', the name used for themselves by the majority of Gypsies in Europe.

Romani The language of the Romanies

Traveller 1 An Irish or Scottish nomad
2 An overall term covering Romany Gypsies as well as Irish and Scottish Travellers

In all quotations the forms 'gipsy' or 'gypsy' have been standardised to 'Gypsy', and 'Traveller' capitalised.

Foreward to the Second Edition

When I first read this book it made a welcome change from the usual reports full of statistics for academics and romantic stories about campfires and hedgehogs. As well as some history and law, there are first hand stories showing what the travelling life is really like – as told by Gypsies themselves.

The situation of our people in England has got worse with new laws and our traditional way of life is under attack. So, I welcome this new edition which is full of valuable information for those who want to understand our problems.

Peter Mercer
Secretary, East Anglian Gypsy Council
Representative of Britain on the Presidium of the World Romany Union.

Introduction to the First Edition

In writing this booklet we were conscious of following in the footsteps of two earlier authors. First, Grattan Puxon wrote – and the NCCL published – *On the Road* (1968) which became a powerful weapon for the emerging Gypsy Civil Rights movement at the time of the Caravan Sites Act. Secondly, Martin Smith whose *Gypsies – Where Now?* (1975) was a Young Fabian pamphlet which influenced the Parliamentary Labour Party leading eventually to a new Caravan Sites Bill which unfortunately never reached the statute book.

Gypsies are again at a crisis point where their survival as an ethnic group is being threatened on all sides while for many families life is no easier than that described twenty-seven years ago in *On the Road*.

In these pages we give a description of the Gypsy population of England as it is, as well as of the stereotypes that abound and show how, although harassed as a minority, they have not, in practice, had the protection which the law should afford to minorities. We list the legislation which has been brought in to control their movements and their relationships with the police as well as local and central government agencies. Finally, we look at the emerging interest the European organisations are taking in their nomad populations.

We would like to acknowledge the help we have had at all stages from Thomas Acton, Peter Mercer and David Rosenberg.

Donald Kenrick, Sian Bakewell

Note
This new edition has been prepared by Donald Kenrick and it updates the information to the end of 1994.

Chapter 1   A profile of the Gypsy community

Who are the Gypsies?

The present day Gypsy population of the United Kingdom can be divided into five main groups, each with its own cultural heritage.

1.   The Romanies or 'Romany chals' of England and South Wales. This is the largest group, numbering over 50,000 – including house-dwelling families. They previously spoke a dialect of Romani but now speak a variety of English. They are descendants of Romanies (known as 'Egyptians') who came to England from the Continent in the 16th and 17th centuries. There has, of course, been some intermarriage with English people, but earlier customs are still preserved. In particular, different sorts of washing are kept separate, and often the possessions of the dead are burnt or otherwise destroyed.

2.   The Kalé of North Wales. Some 300 persons, descendants of the Woods and other families who migrated from the south-west of England to Wales in the 17th and 18th centuries. Up to a few years ago they spoke inflected Romani (with endings changing for tense and case).

3   The Roma – Gypsies who have come to England this
     century. They include Coppersmiths whose grandparents
     came here in the 1930s and Hungarian Gypsies, most of
     whom arrived as refugees after 1956. The majority now
     live in houses but the women still wear the traditional
     long dresses and ornaments. The Coppersmiths, at least,
     keep up Romani as their main language while telling
     neighbours they are Greeks, to avoid discrimination.

The term 'Gypsy' in the 1968 Caravan Sites Act includes two
other nomadic groups:

4   Irish Travellers. These are a nomadic group from
     Ireland. Some say they are the descendants of peasants
     driven off their lands by Cromwell but there is historical
     and linguistic evidence for placing their origin as a
     separate ethnic group much earlier, even before the
     coming of the Celts to Ireland. They now speak a variety
     of English.
         It is estimated that 8,000 are in England, the majority
     in caravans. Although Irish immigration to England
     began several centuries ago the first reliable report of
     the presence of Irish Travellers dates from 1850. After
     the Second World War many men came over to work on
     the motorways and later as labourers for local councils,
     as well as scrap metal dealers. Travelling women could
     pass as ordinary Irish and get work in hospitals, which
     was not so easy in Ireland itself because of prejudice. On
     the whole the Irish Travellers have found it more
     difficult to get on local authority caravan sites.

5   Scottish Travellers. These are a nomadic group formed in
     Scotland in the period 1500-1800 from intermarriage and
     social integration between local nomadic craftsmen and
     immigrant Gypsies from France and Spain in particular.
     As many as 2,000 Scottish Travellers may visit England
     each year in caravans for stays of varying lengths. These
     and the New Age Travellers have not been included in
     the table overleaf.

Table A: Population figures
Overall numbers of Gypsies of each ethnic group in England

	Total	In caravans	In houses
Romanies	53,000	27,000	26,000
Irish Travellers	8.000	6,000	2,000
Roma	2,000	50	1,950
Scots Travellers	200		200
Kalé	50		50
Totals (to nearest 1,000)	63,000	33,000	30,000

A brief history
North-west India formed the cradle of the Romany nation. This much at least is accepted by all those who have attempted to reconstruct the history of the Gypsy people. Possibly they existed as a loose confederation of nomadic craftsmen and entertainers following a pattern similar to groups such as the Banjara and Sapera (Kalbelia) in modern India. Possibly such a confederation formed during their stay in the Middle East. There are no contemporary accounts of the first Romanies to reach Persia but the poet Firdausi and other writers in the tenth century write of the arrival of Indian entertainers five hundred years earlier. Linguistic and other evidence suggests that the Gypsies of Europe belong to groups which left India over a thousand years ago. They spent a comparatively short time in the Middle East. At no time did they move in a solid mass from east to west but their pattern of migration was probably similar to that of today with one family group overtaking another, according to local circumstances and opportunity for work.

They came to eastern Europe from Asia Minor early in the fourteenth century. The first families recorded earned their living as shoemakers and metalworkers. Eastern Europe has continued to have a large settled Romany population, in contrast to western Europe where the word 'Gypsy' is synonymous with 'nomad.' The first authenticated records of their presence in Britain are in 1505 for Scotland and 1514 for Lambeth in England. However, since two ladies apparently dressed up as Gypsies for a court masked ball in

England as early as 1510 it is likely that the real Gypsies had been in the country for some years before then.

The common people welcomed these newcomers who performed many useful services in town and country or provided entertainment as a welcome relief from dull everyday life. However, the Gypsies soon aroused the hostility of powerful enemies. The Church resented the competition of palm readers, the Guilds the fact that the Gypsies could undercut their prices and the State wanted them to settle down, register their names and birthdates and occupy a fixed position in the system. Soon after their arrival the English Parliament passed an Act under which all 'Egyptians' in the country were to leave within sixteen days and further immigration was prohibited. Later legislation introduced the death penalty. The extent to which these laws were applied varied from one part of the country to the other but men and women were executed in Aylesbury, Durham and York for the sole crime of 'being a Gypsy'.

After 1780 anti-Gypsy legislation was gradually repealed. Tolerated when they were useful as farm labour, blacksmiths or entertainers, made to move on when their services were no longer needed, the Gypsies survived on the margins of society until the outbreak of World War II.

With the outbreak of war and subsequent conscription of able-bodied men and women the Gypsies became a useful source of labour for the war effort. Men were called up to the army and women recruited for land work and the munitions factories. Unable to read and travelling from place to place many young men never received their 'call-up papers'. Police rounded them up. Once in uniform, Gypsies, as in the First World War, fought heroically, winning many medals. They were particularly valued as snipers and scouts, both in Europe and the Far East.

There was a dark side too. A soldier might come home on leave to find the caravan site had been broken up by the police and he had to return to barracks not knowing where his family was, whether they were still alive or perhaps had been killed in a bombing raid.

It is often forgotten that, in addition to the Jews, Nazi

Germany tried to wipe out Gypsies, homosexuals, socialists, trades unionists, Jehovah's Witnesses and persons with disabilities. Some Gypsies were aware that across the Channel Hitler's Germany was planning to annihilate them. In 1942, preparatory to a planned invasion of Britain, the Central Security Office in Berlin started to collect information on the Gypsy population of England.

After 1945 there was a brief period when Gypsies were able to live at peace with their house-dwelling neighbours. The coming to power of a Labour Government brought a new tolerance generally towards minorities, there was plenty of work for all with reconstruction after the war and, with many bombed-out or demobilised families living in prefabricated houses or mobile homes, the Gypsies in their caravans were no longer an anomaly. However, within a few years a shortage of land arose and led to problems as we shall see below.

It was not long before governments of both parties began to try and control immigration, including that of Gypsies. In July 1966, for example, fifteen families coming from the Continent with caravans were stopped at Southampton and sent back to Europe. There are records of two other large groups being refused entry in 1970 and 1975. Since the setting-up of the European Community, Gypsies from western Europe have the right to come here. However, this does not mean the right to a place on a caravan site or to ply their traditional trades as they cannot obtain pedlars' licences without which they cannot sell in the street or from house to house.

Many Gypsies found themselves stateless after World War II. The United Kingdom signed the Convention on Stateless Persons (1954) which states "The contracting states shall as far as possible facilitate the assimilation and naturalisation of stateless persons".

In practice the Home Office ignores this convention. To take one case of many. Mr K. was a stateless nomad. His parents who had been born in Poland, where their birth was not registered, came to Spain in the 1930s where Mr.K was born. He arrived in the United Kingdom with a temporary

Spanish travel document, which was stolen along with all his money soon after arrival. Befriended by some local Gypsies, he stayed with them and worked in their family business. When he decided to come up from 'underground' and ask for permission to reside here the UK Government tried to deport him first to Spain, whose government refused entry, and then to Poland. The Home Office remained adamant:

"The existence of the Committee of Experts on Stateless Nomads on which the United Kingdom is represented and the Council of Europe's resolutions on stateless nomads do not preclude stateless nomads from the requirement to qualify to enter or remain in the United Kingdom under the Immigration Rules. The recommendations of the Council of Europe about nomads do not, in our view, put them in a special position in relation to the exercise of immigration control. We will continue to treat nomad applicants no more or less favourably than anyone else."

In recent years Romanies from eastern Europe have tried to get asylum because of racial attacks in their own countries. The attitude of the Home Office is that there may be 'harassment' of Gypsies but this does not amount to 'persecution' so the applicants are refused and sent back to where they came from. Only a small number holding Yugoslav papers and unable to return to Bosnia because of the fighting have been allowed to stay.

Work
Success in most European countries is viewed in terms of career achievements. This, however, is not the case in Gypsy society where work is considered not to be an end in itself but a means of earning money while staying independent. Independence requires mobility and adaptability. The Gypsies have the power to adjust and have adapted their trades successfully to growing industrialisation. Gypsies, therefore, rarely have one single occupation but practice a combination of trades, such as scrap collecting, tarmacking, hawking, fortune-telling and so on. These trades also require

minimum equipment which enables them to stay mobile.

In contrast with sedentary people, Gypsies have until now not sought a fixed employment as this would hinder their freedom. They generally work as a domestic or family unit and will, therefore, rarely have the need to employ others. This domestic unit of production also enables them to avoid becoming employees which would entail sedentarisation. Sedentarisation can occur at either end of the economic scale. When prosperous, a Gypsy may open a business such as a scrap yard or plant nursery which in turn demands the employment of labour and a fixed abode. Also when destitute or tied to a site with no work area a Gypsy may have to resort to wage labour employment.

Seasonal work provides an ideal source of income. Particularly in rural areas where fruit and vegetable pickers are still needed, Gypsies constitute an ideal labour force. They appear when work needs doing and disappear when it is finished. They provide their own accommodation and are not likely to go on strike for high wages.

Patterns of movement and work vary, which cut down on competition from other Gypsies but it is dangerous to generalise. However, traditionally, Gypsies winter in one place and may then set off shortly after Easter for early farm work, such as picking daffodils in the West Country and touring around to see when soft fruit is likely to be ready. June brings Epson Races for fortune-telling and dealing or just meeting friends and relatives. Some may then go to Appleby or Cambridge Midsummer Fair – but many of the traditional fairs, such as Yarm Fair, have been closed down. There may be work to be found at the seaside, telling fortunes for the women, moving deck chairs by lorry for the men. Otherwise a dry summer is ideal for repairing roofs, landscape gardening, gate making and so on. Autumn brings a chance for plum and potato picking and then back to the edge of a town to seek a suitable site for the winter.

Work patterns distinguish the Gypsy and Travelling people from other groups. There may be other migrant workers but rarely do these remain as independent of wage labour as the Gypsies. However, although independent of wage labour they do depend upon the demand of the house-dwelling population for the goods and services they supply.

Unfortunately, nomadism combined with the avoidance of conventional employment and their dependence on the sedentary population, has conjured up the stereotype of the Gypsies as parasites. This is unfounded as there has to be a demand for the Gypsies to supply and both sides benefit from these transactions.

In caravans and houses

Nomadism is perhaps the most notable feature of Gypsy lifestyle in Britain and one that has perhaps created the most misunderstanding. The myth of the 'wandering Gypsies', alien everywhere they roam, has hounded them in the past in every country through which they have travelled. This nomadism is in contrast with modern European society where the populace remains largely sedentary.

Not all Romany Gypsies are nomads and not all nomads are Romany Gypsies and a Gypsy is not merely a member of a wandering race as defined by the *Oxford English Dictionary*. Some Gypsies live by the seasons, as we wrote above. They may remain sedentary in the winter months and then travel in the spring, while others may stay in the same place for several years, moving only ten or fifteen times in their lives. Yet others move all the time with occupations requiring a continual supply of new customers. Some travel throughout the British Isles while others will never leave a particular county. Nomadism is a state of mind rather than a state of action. Even when sedentary a Gypsy remains a nomad in his values and spirit. If he buys a bungalow he may well keep a small touring caravan in the backyard, just in case. A Gypsy settled in a house is still called a Traveller for, in addition to its practical functions, nomadism is a part of Gypsy identity and distinguishes them from the 'Gorgios'.

Nomadism has helped them to safeguard their culture by enabling them to avoid too much contact with the non-Gypsy. They travel not because they are asocial or antisocial but because travel is part of their heritage. In the debate leading up to the 1968 Caravan Sites Act Parliament accepted this and proposed the setting up of a national network of sites between which Gypsies could move and preserve their way of life. Many Gypsies moved onto these sites but now stay put because there is nowhere for them to move to, as there are insufficient pitches. Table C shows that between 3,000-4,000 Traveller families have nowhere to stop.

This lack of room on authorised caravan sites and the consequent harassment they encounter on roadside encampments is a major problem for Gypsies in England and Wales today. A possible alleviation of this could be the trend of Gypsies moving into houses. A 1987 Department of the Environment report by Elizabeth Davies shows that during 1985 a significant number of Gypsies moved into houses (see table B below). No later figures are available.

For centuries the nomadic life style of the Gypsies has been one cause of dislike (tinged perhaps with jealousy) and suspicion. Settling and assimilating the Gypsies is a means of lessening the distinction between them and the majority population, a means of rendering this 'strange' people normal.

Local authorities have at times attempted settlement policies to alleviate the 'Gypsy problem'. Some have been well-intentioned and have aimed at improving the poor conditions which Gypsies have to endure. The Davies' report takes one such example of settlement in the centres set up in the 1960s by Hampshire County Council. Many Gypsies took advantage of these centres which provided them initially with low grade accommodation. If they showed a willingness to assimilate to house-dwelling society by abandoning their dogs and their distinctive clothing, normal council housing accommodation was offered.

In other cases local authorities have been reluctant to accommodate those Gypsies who wish to be housed although the Homeless Persons Act gives them this duty in the case of any Gypsy without a legal pitch. A London council demanded that one family (who had registered as homeless) stay on their illegal site until the bailiffs (acting under the order of the same council) arrived, then leave their caravan and report to the Housing Office. Even if families are technically ruled to be 'intentionally homeless' they can now be housed under certain sections of the Children Act.

This reluctance to house Gypsies is, in some cases, due to fear of hostility by the local population towards their future Gypsy neighbours. Of greater importance in the comparatively low take-up of housing are the psychological problems which they may face at the prospect of permanent housing. Housing takes away the freedom and mobility which are major features of Gypsy life in England today. There are further problems in working from a house. A Gypsy was refused permission to conduct a car valeting service in his extensive grounds, although the nearest neighbour was a lorry park on the opposite side of the road. Another has not been allowed to park a lorry next to his new home.

If entered into for positive reasons, such as stable education for the children or a more secure environment for their elderly parents, housing can be successful. It seems, however, that a large proportion of those Gypsies who go into housing do so for negative reasons, to escape harassment or as a result of poverty. As Elizabeth Davies points out, the help of local authority workers to make the transition into housing a smooth one is often not available and the result is that many Gypsies leave housing within a short period of time and return to the road.

Table B: Moving into housing
Number of families who moved into housing

	From authorised sites	From unauthorised sites	Total
1981-5	248	275	523
1985	84	112	196

Number of families moving out of housing (1981-5) 146

From E. Davies, *Gypsies and Housing*. Department of Environment, 1987.

Chapter 2 Gypsies and race relations – theory and practice

Blacks, Gypsies and Jews

Since their arrival in Europe, Blacks, Gypsies and Jews have often shared persecution. Arriving later than the Jews, the Gypsies could not be accused, as were the former, of spreading the Black Death, although they were blamed for an outbreak of bubonic plague in Italy.

It has been said that the Gypsies were 'the first Blacks in Europe'. The Romanies, dark-skinned as they were, aroused colour prejudice towards people with skins other than pink. In Romania and other parts of the Balkans they were forced into serfdom in their hundreds under rules more severe than for the local feudal serfs. They could be bought and sold, families were split up, while runaway Gypsies were tortured if recaptured just as the black slaves in the Americas. Gypsies in Romania were not emancipated until the 19th century.

In Spain expulsion orders were issued almost simultaneously against Gypsies, Jews and Moors. In England Queen Elizabeth acted against "Blackamoors" and "Egyptians". The former "shall with all speed be avoided and discharged out of this her Majesty's dominions". As for the latter she added the death penalty for Gypsies who disobeyed an earlier order to leave the country, at the same time as she executed her doctor, the only Jew left in London after an earlier expulsion.

Many Gypsies remained as they had nowhere else to go, some found safety by working for nobles and landowners but others were arrested and executed. York, scene of the death of forty Jews in the thirteenth century, was to witness a mass execution of Gypsies in 1596. Gypsies, however, through their nomadism were able to survive in a Britain where the forces of law were not nationally organised.

At the end of the nineteenth century Jewish and Gypsy immigrants arrived from Eastern Europe. In 1906 Major Gordon Evans spoke against German Gypsies' who were trying to settle in England. He was the same MP who had organised opposition to Jewish immigration the previous year culminating in the Aliens Act.

It is not surprising that Zionism has its echo amongst the Romanies, giving impetus to the idea of Romanestan, a Gypsy national home. Janusz Kwiek, leader of the Coppersmith tribes in Poland before 1939 came to London and spoke in Hyde Park to seek support for his proposals for a homeland in Africa. After 1945 Vaida Voevod (see section 5 below) wrote to the United Nations asking for help in getting land in India. But most Gypsies now feel like the poet Ronnie Lee: "Romanestan is where my two feet stand" and try to keep an independent cultural existence in the various countries where they live.

For the Nazis in Germany Jews, Gypsies and 'Negroes' were the only foreign element in the state. For the extreme right in Britain today all three are enemies, though anti-semitism is less open.

Gypsies are a race

The Court of Appeal in 1988 confirmed that 'Gypsies', in the original sense of Romanies, are legally recognised in Britain as an ethnic group. The judgment arose from a court case (CRE v. Dutton) in which the Commission for Racial Equality (CRE) accused a publican in East London of discrimination because he had put a notice outside his pub reading "No Travellers served".

The CRE maintained that Travellers was a synonym for Gypsies and the notice therefore discriminated against

Gypsies who are a racial group. The Appeal Court ruled that Gypsies are indeed an ethnic group. Because they have a common history, culture, oral literature and practices of a religious nature they fit the so-called Mandla criteria (established in the House of Lords when it was decided that Sikhs were an ethnic group). Unlike the Saxons and the Vikings they have not been absorbed into the English nation. This gives Gypsies protection under the Race Relations Act and the provisions against incitement to racial harassment of the Public Order Act. A notice reading 'no Gypsies served' is discriminatory.

However, the Appeal Court held that the word 'Traveller' was not a synonym of 'Gypsy' but referred to a wider group, including non-Romany Travellers and 'New Age Gypsies'. They did not accept the CRE's argument that this wider group was itself an ethnic group within the Mandla criteria. A notice "No Travellers served" indirectly discriminates against Romanies but it is not illegal if some justification can be given for refusing to serve Travellers as a whole.

The roots of prejudice
From the time of their first appearance in Britain, Gypsies can be compared with modern immigrants from East Africa and Asia. They came in small family groups seeking opportunities to carry on existing trades and occupations among settled populations. There was little space for them and no chance to establish, even if they had wanted to, their own settlements and homeland as, for example, the Vikings had done before them. Every territory had already been allocated to a nobleman or city dwelling merchant.

The only place for the Gypsies was, therefore, on the fringes of society where they had to make a living as best as they could. The fact that they were nomads, travelling with carts and tents, had its advantages and disadvantages. They could move to seek new markets and to avoid trouble but they did not stay in any one place long enough to build up a relationship with the local people.

Stereotypes

Stereotyped images of the Gypsies have appeared throughout their history. They provide the basis for persecution and serve to rationalise the measures taken against them. Since their arrival in Europe Gypsies have suffered particularly from two contradictory false images. The image of the mysterious and attractive wanderer, the romantic violin-playing lover or the seductive dancer has been intermixed with the image of the repulsive and dirty vagabond. False images and stereotypes can be found in everyday language. They are reinforced in the media, in popular literature and children's books.

The *Encyclopaedia Britannica* (in the now superseded 1956 edition) wrote: "The mental age of an average adult Gypsy is thought to be about that of a child of ten."

These stereotypes merely reflect and reinforce what is already widespread in public opinion. Stereotypes of the dirty vagabond are justified by, for example, stories of petty thefts, the nature of the act being more important than the monetary value, and the theft itself being the only way of eating when constant harassment or discrimination prevent normal money-earning activities. The same image is reinforced by photographs in local newspapers of Gypsies up to their knees in rubbish. But people fail to realise, or to admit, that this is because they are living on unhealthy and inadequate sites. Gorgios also fail to realise that the Gypsies have a high code of cleanliness, without which they would never have been able to survive in such unfit conditions.

Thus, not only does the image serve to rationalise the measures taken but the measures in turn reinforce the image. This vicious circle provides the basis for further violations of the Gypsies human rights.

Women

The image of the enticing and sexually provocative Gypsy dancer, as illustrated by Merimée's nineteenth century story *Carmen* is still a feature of modern thought. Today's stereotype is usually romantic, a dark-haired beautiful girl, dressed in rather shabby but flowing fabrics, swinging her hips as she moves. Seduction is the key idea, the Great Temptress. Every few years the 'Romany' motif hits the fashion pages However, once aged, the Gypsy woman becomes an evil old crone with dangerous supernatural powers. Thus either young or old, Gypsy women are never visualised as normal.

The romantic image of the young Gypsy woman is in total contrast to the derogatory stereotype of the Gypsy male. The reason for this is that a handsome Gypsy male would be a potential threat to the houses-dwelling family, as illustrated in D. H. Lawrence's story *The Virgin and the Gypsy*. So, as a rule the Gypsy male is portrayed as a dirty thief and vagabond which lessens this threat. It is not, however, necessary to degrade the image of the Gypsy woman as, in our patriarchal society, women do not pose a threat; the Gorgio man is considered to have a much greater self-control and to be able to resist seduction.

When we examine the role which women play within the Gypsy community it becomes clear that the stereotype is incorrect. At home, Gypsy women must live up to a great many expectations. Rather than seduction, sex before marriage is condemned as is adultery even to the extent that a married woman should not be on her own with a man.

In the media

The popular and local press often run stories on Gypsies, usually with sensational headlines.

CAMP SITE VANDALISED BY GYPSIES
1,600 SAY NO GYPSIES HERE
GYPSY WOMEN HURT IN FEUD
ROMANY HUNTED FOR VICIOUS KILLING
FURY AT YES TO TRAVELLERS SITE
GYPSIES RUIN KIDS SOCCER PITCH
GYPSY SITE SHOCK FOR FARMER
FURY AT CARAVANS ON COMMON
GYPSY CAMP THREAT TO SHEEP FARM
GYPSIES CAUSE TRAFFIC CHAOS

The *Hornsey Journal* of 6 November 1987 printed a picture of rubbish on an illegal site, accompanied by a leading article:

"At a time when kiddies' playgrounds are being closed down and the cost of old people's meals is being increased, Haringey Council is spending half a million pounds on building a permanent Travellers' site and a further £400,000 on running its gay and lesbian committee."

Whether Romany or Irish, the papers don't like Travellers. In 1987 *The Universe* interviewed a local parish priest under the heading.

"TRAINED THIEVES CASH IN ON UNDERGROUND PASSENGERS

Father K. said: 'I suspect most of these people are Travellers. They are not very popular around here. They thieve and get drunk and smash up pubs. The kids are uncontrollable. Some Travellers are squatting in houses that are needed by homeless people.' "

Brochures issued by tour operators reinforce the message.

"PICKPOCKETS

The most skilful thieves are groups of Gypsy children who roam the main tourist areas of Paris and the Metro. Do not stop if approached by these children and never take out your purse or wallet to give them anything as it is likely to be snatched." From Thomsons Guide Book.

"In Mallorca as in all tourist locations all over the world we have a problem with thieves. Here, the Gypsies are the offenders. Don't buy any jewellery or flowers or clothes from them. Gypsies in Mallorca are all professional pickpockets". From Airtours brochure.

In children's books

A false image of the Gypsy is imprinted in children from an early age. Heard in the school playground as a skipping rhyme and still found in nursery rhyme books is the warning:

*My mother said
I never should
play with the Gypsies
in the wood.*

The only book mentioning Gypsies found for the nursery age (3-5) in a recent survey was *Topsy and Tim's Friday Book* where Mother decides that her two children shall dress up as Gypsies for a fancy dress party. They put on something looking vaguely like a Spanish flamenco dancer's dress and win first prize. Children who had this book read to them in the school where it was found in the library would not connect the pictures with the Gypsy women in the campsite up the road from the school.

For the primary school, there are now some good non-fiction books. Many, however, generalise, such as *Gypsies and Nomads* which leaves the impression that all Gypsies have trained bears that dance to a tambourine. The song *The Raggle Taggle Gypsies* reinforces the stereotype of the handsome Gypsy luring away the Gorgio lady (though the original Scottish ballad has a Gorgio lord luring away a Gypsy girl and then locking her up so *she* cannot go back).

Standard works on history, geography and social studies for the secondary school rarely mention Gypsies. A check on the indexes of ten such works in a London library for teachers produced the following figures.

References to
Afro-Caribbeans or West Indians	10
Jews	6
Asians (including Indians and Pakistanis)	4
Gypsies or Romanies	0

The same Centre had on its shelves *Tales and Legends of the Serbians* which describes Gypsies as cunning persons whose main occupation is stealing and selling horses, but none of the recent studies of Gypsies were in the education or sociology sections.

Children's comics still portray male Gypsies as spies, kidnappers or thieves while the Gypsy girl is often a frustrated ballet dancer whose parents will not let her go to school and who has to be smuggled into the classroom by well-wishing schoolgirls.

A recent study of children's fiction by Dennis Binns shows how the myths are still current. Gypsies steal things: "I lost it in town. I know it. This little Gypsy thief stole it from me." And children: "Very likely of noble birth and stolen by Gypsies and stained brown and now they are afraid of pursuit and have left it." (From *The Slowcoach*.)

The standard classics read by older children and adults reinforce the stereotypes. Hugo's *Notre Dame de Paris* (filmed as *The Hunchback of Notre Dame*) has a girl stolen at birth by Gypsies, as does Cervantes' *La Gitanilla* (the Gypsy Girl). Heathcliffe in *Wuthering Heights* is another villain while in Lawrence's *The Virgin and the Gypsy* (also a film) we have the eternal seducer.

Prejudice in practice – opposition to sites
We find ourselves today still with two stereotyped images of the Gypsy. The romantic image, the 'real Gypsy' who is living somewhere else or who died out in the 19th century and the 'dirty Gypsy' who is the one asking for a caravan site in the neighbourhood. The first hint of a proposal for a site brings out the petitions and the public meetings, the 'Residents Action Group' and the same arguments.

The expressed reasons for opposing a site are that Gypsies don't pay rates and taxes and leave a mess. House values will go down (the same argument is used against a hostel for ex-psychiatric patients), the school will be overcrowded (the same argument is used against a new council estate). Sometimes the Gypsies' own welfare is invoked. It's too near a main road and the children would get run over, the Gypsies would be unhappy in a middle class area ...

One reason may be envy. The Gypsies on the illegal site in the corner of the park don't seem to work from nine to five, women and children bob in and out of each other's caravans in a way unknown to those watching from the windows of the high-rise flats nearby and, if they want, they can hitch up their caravans and go to the other end of the country without asking anyone.

Prejudice often turns to violence against an illegal site that seems to be becoming permanent, or 'tolerated' to use the terminology of government circulars.

In 1968 Gypsies came to Greenland Road in Sheffield. Fifty local residents attacked the camp. The Gypsies moved twice, ending up in Tinsley Park. Local residents produced a petition accusing the Gypsies of "nude bathing in the boating lake and allowing horses to mate in public". In July a mob of 200 marched on the caravans and had to be persuaded to return home by the newly-elected Conservative Councillor for the area.

In Kent a youth club leader led a gang which threw a fire bomb at caravans. He was later caught and sent to prison. Shots were fired at another caravan in Kent so regularly that the owner bought a tall van which he placed between his home and the road to protect it.

Near Bedford in 1970 a paving stone was thrown through the window of a caravan, narrowly missing a young girl in bed.

These incidents have continued. This year there were several attacks on Gypsy caravans returning south from Appleby Fair.

Here are a selection of the arguments that have been made against sites either in the press or written submissions to councils:

"If the proposal goes through I will be forced to give up farming because of the problems that would arise from stray dogs from the camp." (Kent)

"The close proximity of these people of possibly Irish origin to the Royal Armament Establishment is a real risk." (Kent)

"The presence of Travellers means higher insurance rates for us, difficulties in attracting clients to our business, difficulties in attracting employees and rubbish everywhere." (Hackney)

"I myself would be extremely concerned about the welfare of the children in my care and would not like to guarantee their safety at all times." (Teacher in Essex)

When a properly run local authority site does open, the previous fears are usually seen to be unjustified.

Even the proposal for a Romany Museum encountered vitriolic opposition. Again these are extracts from submissions to the local council.

"I object to this proposal as Gypsies are filthy, they bring filth and they leave filth. They are thieves and they pay for nothing. I pay rates, I pay tax and my house is clean. The price of my house would be devalued and I would physically participate in removing them. We don't want them here ever."

"A Gypsy museum ... encourage the visitation in large and regular quantities of Gypsies, Travellers, itinerants and other unsavoury characters from all over the Country. Waltham Abbey will deteriorate into a slum area."

The proposal for the Museum was rejected by an Inspector from the Department of the Environment as unsuitable for the area.

Incitement to racial hatred
Sections of the Race Relations Act and the Public Order Act of 1936 cover incitement to racial hatred. There have been few prosecutions since 1939 under the Public Order Act and none in cases concerning Gypsies.

Sections of the Public Order Act of 1986 update the Public Order Act of 1936, an Act originally designed to cover anti-semitic propaganda. During the debate in the House of

Lords in October Lord Elwyn-Jones twice tried to get an amendment into the Bill to clarify that 'Gypsies are a group of persons defined by reference to race'. He cited the CRE which had told him that about a third of the complaints it receives are about hate literature relating to Gypsies.

"They are among the most abused and insulted people in this country. Indeed the language is cruder and more offensive than literature relating to Blacks or Jews which has been or is being prosecuted."

The Earl of Caithness, rejected the amendment, but affirmed:

"We are concerned to see that written material which stirs up racial hatred against Gypsies who are of a distinct ethnic group should be penalized in the same way as any other ethnic or racial group ... When there is evidence that activity of the kinds penalized by Part III (of the Act) has been directed against them my right honourable friend the Attorney General has authorised me to say that he will consider instituting proceedings in exactly the same way as he would in respect of any other ethnic group."

An individual Gypsy cannot take action under this Act. The case has to be reported to the police and then the Attorney General can prosecute. Heartened by the debate in the House of Lords, Eli Frankham of the National Romany Rights Group tried once again to get action over a leaflet which had been circulated in Norfolk.

"GYPSIES AT TILNEY FOR EVER
Without consultation Norfolk County Council is proposing a permanent Gypsy site at Tilney. It may not be at the bottom of your garden but it will affect you as if it were.
YOUR PROPERTY WILL BE DEVALUED
AS MUCH AS 50%
WILL YOU BE HAPPY ABOUT LEAVING YOUR
PROPERTY UNATTENDED?
WILL YOUR SCHOOL REMAIN AT THE

SAME HIGH STANDARD?
THE DOGS – THE RUBBISH – THE SMELL –
THE SCRAP – THE RODENTS
Remember if we don't harass the Council now
we shall be harassed for the rest of our lives."

In 1985 the Solicitor-General had written that he was not satisfied that the leaflet infringed the 1936 Act and that he did not propose to do anything about it. Following the House of Lords debate Mr Frankham wrote again. This time it was the Attorney General's Chambers who replied.

"The assurance given by the Attorney General in the Committee Stage of the (1986) Public Order Bill does not I regret alter the decision made in the matter to which you refer. It has always been the case that there may be circumstances where Gypsies may be considered an ethnic group for the purposes of section 5A of the Public Order Act 1936. However, in order to establish that the 'Gypsies' referred to were an ethnic group, it must be shown that the reference was to true Romany Gypsies, rather than Travellers, tinkers etc."

So to sum up the working of the 1986 Public Order Act: the 'trespass' clause was not intended to apply to Gypsies, but was being used against them daily, while the 'incitement to racial hatred' provisions were intended to help Gypsies but in practice they won't.

In 1970 the Conurbation Action Groups in the Midlands distributed leaflets during the local elections.

"Consider the facts before you give your (X)

TINKERS
Extensive areas invaded by Irish Tinkers. Elderly citizens and communities terrorized. Industry and Commerce subjected to the Highest Crime Wave on record. Provide Tinker Sites and in doing so solve the Republic of Ireland's Tinker Problem."

The leaflet went on to deal with the danger of mixing white and black races.

"To voice concern for England and our families is to be labelled Nazis. We say it will be Mr Benn and his Party, not Enoch Powell, that flies the swastika and constructs the concentration camps obviously to intern all English patriots who dare oppose Labour's Doctrine of a Compulsory Multiracial State".

In 1986 Leeds City Council advertised the following post.

"Assistant Gypsy Liaison Officer/Clinic Attendant to assist in the enforcement of the Council's policies on Gypsies. Additionally the person will assist in the Clinic in the treatment of male clients, frequently vagrants, for lice, fleas, scabies and similar conditions."

Complaints were made about the tone of this advertisement by Gypsy civil rights groups and individuals. The CRE began an action against the City Council but did not pursue it. Although unpleasant it was not incitement to racial hatred. Leeds Council remained unmoved by the protests and no apology was forthcoming. Mr Rawnsley, Chief Officer, replied.

"The Council did reissue the advertisement in question to make it perfectly plain that the two functions of the post advertised i.e. Assistant Gypsy Liaison Officer and Assistant Attendant at the Disinfestation Clinic were entirely separate and simply a question of working practice."

Searchlight has reported harassment by Fascists of a Gypsy boxer and a later racist leaflet, this time in Oldham, while a National Front march in Lewisham included on its route the local Gypsy site. Gypsies defending the site were arrested and charged with assault.

Chapter 3　The struggle for sites

The disappearing *Atching Tan* (stopping place)
We noted earlier that there was a short period after 1945
where Gypsies led a comparatively untroubled life in
harmony with the house-dwelling community for whom they
provided useful services. Two factors were to change this.
First, the movement of their 'customers' from the country to
towns, which had started with industrialisation as early as
1850, gathered speed. This meant that Gypsies too had to
move into towns in order to earn their living but in the towns
they found it harder to find stopping places and also came
into contact with local police and council officials who were
not used to seeing a Gypsy caravan amongst the willow herb
on their old bomb site. They had not met Gypsies before and
had no sympathy for their life style.

The second factor was the conflict over land use,
especially in the south-east. Empty plots in otherwise built
up areas were bought up and built on, disused aerodromes –
popular stopping places since 1945 because of the concrete
runways – were taken over for new housing or industrial
estates, motorways with no grass verges replaced roads, the
prefabricated houses and mobile homes which many Gypsies
had bought and used as a home base after 1945 became
dilapidated and an eyesore to local councillors who wanted
them replaced by the newly popular high rise flats.

Moving on

The reality of moving on is described here in two of a collection of similar accounts presented to the Government by the then Gypsy Council.

"I was expecting one of my babies and my son ran for the midwife. The policeman told us: 'Get a move on, shift on.' My husband said: 'Look sir, let me stay. My wife is going to have a baby.' The policeman answered: 'No, it doesn't matter about that – you get off.' They made my husband move and my baby was born going along the road in my caravan. The horse was in harness and the policeman was following behind".

As their traditional stopping places disappeared Gypsies were moved on by mobile police and council workmen more often and in a more brutal way than by the local country policemen.

"At 8am one morning a Land Rover and a police car arrived. The sergeant hooked up my trailer (caravan). I said there were children inside but he said: 'Never mind the children'. The Land Rover moved forward fast and started along the track at about 15-20mph. Part of the way along the track the Land Rover hit a large pothole. Inside the caravan one of the bunks burst open and our small boy (aged 2) fell from the bunk and onto a nail. When the caravan had been pulled onto the road I asked the sergeant to let me take the boy to hospital for treatment. He refused and insisted I moved or he would charge me with obstruction."

It is in fact illegal to tow a caravan with children inside. The boy was eventually taken to hospital and kept there for several weeks with blood poisoning.

Gypsies may be pulled off with or without a court order, or taken to court and fined. Travelling families stopping on the roadside could be and were prosecuted under a statute dating from 1835. This made it an offence to 'be a Gypsy

encamping on the highway', and was still used until it was
finally repealed in 1980. Under this legislation Gypsies on
the roadside verge or in a layby were committing an offence
while, in theory, a foreign tourist or British holidaymaker
would be able to park a caravan next to them without being
summonsed.

Many local authorities have Local Acts of Parliament,
dating from the 1930s, which give them additional powers.
Thus, the Surrey Act of 1931 enables district councils to draw
a circle of 880 yards radius around any one caravan and ban
any 'movable dwelling' from stopping within that circle for
ever. A Mr G. was fined at Guildford in 1969 under this Act,
for having a chalet (adjudged to be a movable dwelling) on
land which he owned.

A determined policeman can soon drive a family out of
his patch if he wants to. A Gypsy was imprisoned overnight
in Havering for the offence of 'driving a vehicle [his lorry and
caravan] across the pavement' in order to reach a few feet of
anonymous grass to stop for the night, after being evicted in
the morning. The next day he was fined £30 and not
surprisingly moved to the next county. This family has never
been able to get on a site and the children had only a few
days of education from time to time. Early in 1994 the now
grown-up son of this same Gypsy was fined £500 for stopping
on his own land without planning permission.

If all else fails a request to "produce a receipt for every
item in the caravan down to the teaspoons" or be arrested
and taken to court for receiving stolen property will usually
have the desired effect. Local authorities have become more
ingenious in barring off empty pieces of land – ditches, low
barriers on car parks, wooden and metal posts, banks of
earth (often hastily planted with rose bushes) are used to
prevent caravans driving on to any open land. Unions
representing local authority workers have told their members
not to evict Gypsies but councils now employ private firms of
security guards to do this work. With or without court orders,
the majority of the nearly four thousand families still unable
to get onto a site are moved on after a few days or weeks and
have to look for a new place to stop.

The Caravan Sites Act of 1960

In 1960 the Government introduced legislation to control private caravan sites. The new law made it difficult for Gypsies to buy small plots of land and winter on them. Section 1 of the Act spelt this out clearly.

"No occupier of land shall after the commencement of this Act cause or permit any part of the land to be used (as a caravan site) unless he is the holder of a site licence."

And you cannot get a site licence unless you have planning permission. After 1960 anyone buying a piece of land had to get first planning permission and then a site licence before they could put a caravan on it. Exceptions were made for 'established sites' and a number of cases were heard over the following years asking for the recognition that the land had 'established use' as a caravan site. It was not always easy to prove that the site had been in use before 1960. The H. family lost the right to remain on their land near Heathrow Airport because the word of the retired Enforcement Officer as to which side of a hedge caravans had been parked fourteen years earlier was believed rather than the statements of the families themselves. They had been refused planning permission because of the danger of 'low flying aircraft' even though houses had been built in the neighbouring village, not to mention luxury hotels on the edge of the airport. Many years later, the Council realised that it would be cheaper and less trouble to abandon the search for an alternative site and let the families stay where they were.

The existence of a caravan site before 1960 and the obtaining of an Established Use Certificate was still no guarantee that the families would be left alone. Local councils were to take over the sites by compulsory purchase and either keep the Gypsies on as their tenants, as in the case of Harrow Manorway (now called Thistlebrook) in Greenwich and Outwood (Surrey), or evict them and build houses as was to happen in Greenways, also in Surrey.

In addition, other Gypsies were driven onto the roadside as private landowners who previously let them stop on their land could no longer do so as they could not get a site licence. The 1960 Caravan Sites Act is also used against farmers who let Gypsies stay on their land before or after the actual days when they are actually working on the crops.

In and out of Parliament
For many years neither the Lords nor the Commons had discussed the Gypsies but this was to change with the election in 1945 of Norman Dodds as Labour MP for Dartford, which contained several shanty towns on the Thames Marshes. Until his death, twenty years later, he was to campaign in the House of Commons on their behalf.

He helped to set up a Committee with Gypsy and Gorgio members which in 1947 drew up a nine-point *Charter*. Its demands included:
■ a survey to be taken of the number of Romanies and Other Travellers in England and Wales.
■ adequate provision of camps with water, sanitation, ablutions, and communal centre facilies.
■ a suitable scheme for the educating of Gypsy children.
■ consideration given to the practicability of training young Romanies as teachers for the education of Romany children in established camps.

In 1950 Dodds was much moved by an old Gypsy woman from Manchester who had travelled to ask his help. Her husband had been killed in Italy during World War II. She and her daughter had been evicted from the piece of land which they owned and had lived on for over twenty years until a Compulsory Purchase Order had displaced them. For the past two years they had been hounded from place to place. In November of the same year he was to ask the first question on this subject for many years.

"Mr Dodds asked the Minister of Health what steps he is taking to alleviate the serious position that is developing for Gypsies in finding places where they and their caravans can be accommodated.

Mr Bevan (Minister of Health). 'I am considering with my Right Honourable Friend the Home Secretary what information is available to us on this matter and am not yet in a position to say what further steps may be required.'"

It was to be fifteen years before the Government had sufficient information available to them. However, in 1951 Norman Dodds initiated a debate in the Commons and on 9th May Hugh Dalton received a deputation of Gypsies.Then there followed a General Election. Norman Dodds, now an opposition MP, had to turn his attention to the new Housing Minister, Harold Macmillan. Macmillan agreed to a pilot survey in Kent which Dodds later felt was a delaying tactic to keep him quiet.

Meanwhile, Dartford Rural District Council evicted 200 men, women and children from Darenth Wood. The Times was moved to write in a leader of "the victims whose helplessness merits sympathy". From the publicity aroused by the eviction of these families Dr Charles Hill, by then Minister of Housing, agreed to make a national survey of Gypsies.

Meanwhile, things were happening. Norman Dodds himself opened, not without opposition, a private site. The novelist Barbara Cartland built another in Hertfordshire, while the then Strood Council (in Kent) opened one of the earliest local authority sites. Dodds died suddenly in 1965, three years before the passing of a new Caravan Sites Act, which owed much to his endeavours. By then others had joined the struggle.

The Caravan Sites Act of 1968

We referred above to the survey initiated by Charles Hill in 1962. Replies from local councils were voluntary and sparse. In 1964 a new Government took office and a new Minister of Housing, Richard Crossman, decided to get things moving. On 22 March 1965 a national survey of Gypsies took place. It recorded some 15,500 "Gypsies and other Travellers", perhaps 75 per cent of the real number, but a start had been made and the Government and its civil servants could no longer claim, as had Aneurin Bevan in 1950, that there was not enough information available.

The survey report was published in 1967 under the title *Gypsies and Other Travellers*. It found that 60 per cent of the families had travelled in the previous year. In many cases this travelling was not voluntary but the result of harassment by the police and council officials. Few children received any regular schooling. Only 33 per cent of the families had access to a water supply. There were few local authority sites, even though the 1960 Caravan Sites Act had given councils the power to set up caravan sites.

In this same year the Government offered to support Eric Lubbock (later Lord Avebury) with his private bill dealing with the scandalous practices of some private mobile home owners in return for his adding a second part on the subject of Gypsy sites. There has been some debate on whether these provisions were introduced because of, or in spite of, the campaigning of the newly formed Gypsy Council. Thomas Acton (in *Gypsy Politics and Social Change*) analyses this debate and we shall not attempt to improve on his analysis.

The major provisions of the 1968 Caravan Sites Act, as it affected Gypsies, were:

■ County Councils and London Boroughs have a duty to provide accommodation for Gypsies residing in and resorting to their areas.

■ a London Borough need not provide accommodation for more than fifteen caravans. (Section 6)

■ The Secretary of State for the Environment may give directions to any local authority requiring them to provide sites. These directions are enforceable by mandamus. (Section 9)

■ an Area can be designated as an area in which Gypsies cannot station their caravans except if there are pitches free on the official site. It is a criminal offence to do so. (Sections 10 and 11).

Gypsies are defined in the Act as "persons of nomadic

habit of life, whatever their race or origin". This definition has now been moved to the 1960 Act.

The provisions of Section 11 enabled a constable to arrest without warrant anyone who is organising the sort of passive resistance to evictions which the Gypsy Council had encouraged during 1967, while the designation provisions of Section 10 have been compared, with some degree of accuracy, by Gypsy spokespersons as similar to the Pass Laws and apartheid once operating in South Africa. In the following section we look at the working of the 1968 Act.

After the 1968 Act

The 1968 Caravan Sites Act, in so far as it affected Gypsies, came into force on 1st April 1970. Some may consider this a well chosen date as the Gypsies were certainly fooled into thinking there was to be some rapid improvement in their living conditions.

After a two year wait for this part of the Act to come into force, George Marriott and other activists in Bedfordshire organised a celebration of 'Gypsy Independence Day'. Gypsies and supporters came from London and elsewhere, a bonfire was lit, songs were sung and everyone thought that the long years of harassment had ended. In fact, it was to be a hard struggle for Gypsies, their supporters, sympathetic councillors and officials before a realistic number of sites were provided.

Table C below shows what progress had been made by the time we went to press and that several thousand families are still waiting for a site. Children born in 1970 are now twenty five and many of them have, in spite of circulars from the Government urging an end to harassment and the provision of temporary sites, spent these years on the move and unable to get regular schooling.

In particular, district councils have often held up the attempts of county councils to open sites. Worse still the 1960 Caravan Sites Act was used by district councils to get Gypsies off land in their area owned by the county council, even when the county council was following the government recommendations not to harass families. So, in 1972 the now

defunct Caterham and Warlingham Urban District Council
used the 1960 Act to take Surrey County Council to court for
"permitting land to be used as a caravan site without a
licence", that is to say, not evicting some Gypsies parked in a
field in Tupwood Lane. The case was heard at Caterham on
26th June, the barrister representing the Gypsies was not
allowed to address the court as it was ruled that the Gypsies
'had no interest in the matter' and the County Council were
found guilty and fined £40. After a similar case in
Hertfordshire the Government stepped in and now a county
council does not need a licence to run a site. The Department
of the Environment can, however, call in a controversial site
proposal for a public enquiry.

Only for a short period around 1977 while the late
Donald Byrne was Gypsy Sites Officer at the Ministry of
Housing (forerunner of the Department of the Environment)
did central government exert any pressure on councils to set
up sites. The Gypsy Council argued for the immediate setting
up of a chain of temporary but official sites and in areas
where the Council was strong such sites were opened, often
with primitive facilities but at least providing a haven from
police and bailiffs.

The Cripps Report
In 1977 the Government, aware of the shortcomings of the
1968 Act, or rather the way in which local authorities had
ignored its provisions, commissioned John Cripps to make a
rapid one-person study of the workings of the Act. Although
he was not asked to make a detailed study like that which
produced the 1965 Report (*Gypsies and Other Travellers*) he
did, nevertheless, write an impressive document. Following
this the Labour Government introduced a new Caravan Sites
Bill, embodying many of his suggestions. Unfortunately for
the Gypsies this Labour Government was to fall before all
stages of the Bill could get through Parliament. Some of
Cripps' suggestions were later to be incorporated in the 1980
Local Government Act.

Table C: Counts of caravans
Department of Environment figures

	January 1989*	July 1994
Unauthorised encampments	3,740	3,782
Authorised – council	5,159	5,644
Authorised – private	2,422	3,169
Total	11,321	12,595

* Taken from the first edition of this publication.

Designation – Gypsy-free zones
Under the 1968 Act, 'designated' areas of the country are those where Gypsies cannot station a caravan on vacant pieces of land without committing a crime. In 1972 the first designations were proposed – the then County Boroughs of Plymouth, St Helens and Stoke, followed in the same year by Manchester, Richmond on Thames and Wolverhampton. Plymouth has kept its status and the powers that go with it even though it has not had a site for many years. Legally it is a Gypsy-free zone. Apart from a short pause while John Cripps (see above) was reviewing the working of the Act, the process of designation has continued right up to 1994, encompassing whole counties such as Dorset and West Sussex.

What did designation mean in practice? It should mean that all the Gypsies usually resident in an area have been provided with pitches and that there are some pitches in reserve for families 'resorting to' the area for short periods, whether for work or to visit relatives. All Gypsies would have to stop on a site. This would not be unreasonable. In practice it has meant providing the minimum number of pitches that the district can get away with, based on an inadequate census that misses perhaps 10 per cent of families on the roadside and 50 per cent of those on private sites, and then hounding out of the area any caravans that arrive in transit.

In 1986 West Sussex (designated in 1982) claimed, in terms more appropriate to civil war than to a programme of social aid, "to be on the verge of victory in its battle to sweep away unauthorised Gypsy caravan sites from the county's roadsides", as the West Sussex Gazette put it.

Since the county had a duty to provide for any Gypsy families 'residing in or resorting to' the area, we may wonder why there should be any caravans on the roadside at all. At any rate we would hope that the Council was sweeping these families from the roadside on to officially provided sites. However, in the year prior to this statement forty three caravans had come into the county. They were served with summonses immediately and warned that, if they did not move out of the county, court action would be taken.

The Government's decision to designate is apparently infallible. In reply to a letter pointing out that there were still unsited families in the four designated districts of Buckinghamshire, the County Secretary replied,

"Designation would not have been granted for the four districts if the Secretary of State had not at the time been satisfied that the proper provision has been made."

Yet there were thirty three unsited caravans in July 1982 while designation was being considered and a count in March 1983 showed forty on the roadside proper and twelve more squatting on the edge of a full site.

The Government had the power to de-designate an area but this has never been used. Under the proposals in the new Criminal Justice and Public Order Act the powers previously available in designated areas have been strengthened and will apply across the whole of England (and Wales). They will be available against all caravans, probably to stop New Age Travellers from defending any court proceedings by claiming they are not Gypsies.

Life on an Official Site

During the debate on the 1968 Act it was stressed that the intention was to provide 'a network of sites on which the Gypsies could continue their traditional way of life'. In January 1994 there were 303 council-run sites operating, providing some 5,000 pitches. To what extent has the intention of the Act been carried out?

In the first place there are not enough sites or pitches. This in itself brings many problems. Families are afraid to leave a site in order to seek work in case they cannot get a pitch when they want to return. They may then have to move to another site and find a new school for their children, new doctor and so on. More likely they will end up on the roadside or the side of a rubbish tip. A few enlightened authorities do allow Travellers to reserve a pitch on payment of half or full rent for a limited number of weeks each summer.

The least provided for are the 'long-distance' Travellers with their specialised trades such as gate making, who need to travel all the year round. In the past they often stopped on private land and paid rent but the working of the 1960 Act has put a stop to this. Transit sites or transit pitches on residential sites have been suggested in Government circulars. But there is little such provision. The Government set up an enquiry (for which they imported two sociologists from America) and this recommended a chain of Government-run sites along the major motorways. This report (*The Special Accommodation Needs of Long-distance and Regional Travellers*) has been ignored.

The social life of Gypsies has been changed by the way official sites are organised. The most popular number for pitches is sixteen, fifteen caravans and a warden's hut, all neatly marked out with white paint to the same size and numbered. The figure of fifteen is based on the minimum number for which London Boroughs had to provide. In the past Gypsies could choose their own neighbours when they stopped in a field. Now the Council decides who will occupy any vacant pitch on the basis of a points system similar to that used for housing vacancies. Two families from groups which have traditionally been economic rivals may find themselves unwilling neighbours. If in-laws come to visit there are further problems. In the past they would pull up their caravan alongside and while keeping their own cooking and sleeping facilities would be able to enjoy the company of children and grandchildren for a few days. Nowadays they have to leave their own caravan behind and sleep in a perhaps already overcrowded caravan. The same applies to a mother who wants to come and help her daughter before or after a birth or an aged parent that a family would like to have nearby. Caravans arriving to attend a funeral or wedding add to the problems. The old freedom has gone.

No allowance is made either for children growing up. As they get older the family needs two caravans so that sons and daughters can sleep apart. Many councils then insist on a one caravan per pitch rule and so the family has to rent a second pitch – if they can afford it. This pitch may well not be adjacent to the parents' caravan. There has been some friction on sites where one family has tried to create vacancies for other relatives to move on.

Bureaucratic procedures make it difficult to get on a site. These regulations from Nuneaton are typical. An applicant for a pitch has to fill in a two-page form. In addition to what seem to be reasonable requests for information such as details of the caravan, the form asks:

> "How many vehicles do you have at the present time?
> Have you any regular occupation? (give details)
> Name of employer
> Have you occupied any other local authority site?
> If so where?"

After completing the form the applicant apparently has to return to the roadside but keep in touch to find out whether they have been accepted for a pitch. Once on the site they have to abide by the seventeen conditions of this licence from which we give a selection.

> "The licensees shall not keep on the site any animals or poultry with the exception of a single domestic pet for which prior approval is obtained in writing from the Chief Housing Officer."
> "The licensee must produce a certificate of worthiness (in compliance with the Institute of Electrical Engineers) of any electrical installations when required by the Council."
> "The caravan must be of proprietary manufacture and of

an external colour approved by the Council."

In addition to the seventeen conditions of the licence there are eleven 'site regulations' such as:

"No bonfires shall be lit on the site."
"No trade or business shall be carried on on any part of the site other than on vehicles on individual plots."

Any Gypsies who are able and willing to accept these conditions, which mean radically changing their life style, had to pay a deposit of £75 and four weeks rent in advance before being allowed on to the site.

The tenant is allowed to vacate the site for a maximum of four weeks only to do seasonal work – much less than the normal summer agricultural season. While away they have to pay full rent and the Council informs the DSS that the family is away.

Even if the family keep these conditions, they have no security. Caravan sites for Gypsies are specifically excluded from the protection of Part 1 of the 1968 Caravan Sites Act and the Mobile Homes Act. A Council can terminate the licence by giving notice at any time and the caravan family have to leave. They have no recourse to the courts, a point confirmed in a recent judgment by the House of Lords in the case of Greenwich versus Powell. The fact that Mr Powell himself no longer travelled and had lost his Gypsy status did not affect the status of the site. It was built as a Gypsy site and, therefore, the Council had the power to evict any tenant without a reason be they Gypsies or not. The irony of this particular case is that the Greenwich site had originally been privately owned by the Gypsies themselves.

In Bedfordshire a Gypsy single parent was given notice because her brother and his wife had come and parked on their pitch over Christmas without her obtaining permission from the site warden – who was on leave at the time.

Transit sites
The 1968 Act spoke of provision for Gypsies "residing in and resorting to an area". It was assumed that provision for those

'resorting to an area' would mean transit sites or transit pitches so that nomadic families could move around the country in search of work but find a pitch wherever they were. In practice, few local authorities have provided transit pitches. Often transit pitches are converted into permanent pitches to meet the demand for long-term stays.

The Courts and the Ombudsmen

" 'Mandamus' is a judicial writ issued as a command to an inferior court or ordering persons to perform public or statutory duty". (From the Latin for 'we command').

'Mandamus' alongside 'designation' has become an everyday word in the vocabulary of the Gypsy civil rights worker. Under the 1968 Caravan Sites Act the Secretary of State can give directions to any local authority requiring them to provide such sites or additional sites as may be specified in the directions. If the local authority refused then the Secretary of State could apply to a court for a writ of mandamus and then they would have to build these sites or be in contempt of court.

It is only the Secretary of State who can go to court. In the case of Kensington and Chelsea LBC v. Roy Wells (1973) the Court of Appeal ruled that an individual Gypsy had no right to go to court in order to compel a local authority to build a site, under Section 9(2) only the Minister could do so. Bill Forrester, in the standard work on the law as it affects Gypsies, wonders why – with all the amendments there have been to the 1968 Act – Section 9(2) has been retained. Could it be a deliberate move to protect local authorities and the courts from a series of cases by dissatisfied Gypsies? An individual can, however, ask the High Court for a Judicial Review of any decision of a local authority, whether to close a site or not to open one and a number of cases have been heard. A 1983 case, also involving Kensington, confirmed this point. The most important decision since has been the West Glamorgan case in 1986.

"It was held on appeal that the decision of September 1985 by West Glamorgan County Council to evict Gypsies from a place called Briton Ferry was 'perverse'. Further that the Council should not seek possession of the site until they had made reasonable alternative provision for the accommodation of Gypsies."

With the removal by the new Criminal Justice Act of of the duty on county councils to provide sites this ruling may not stand, though a more recent case (South Hams v. Rolls) suggests that even districts – who had no duty under the l1968 Act – may have a moral duty towards Gypsies.

In December 1988 the Secretary of State issued a direction to Hertfordshire to provide more sites, but with no time limit. The power of mandamus in the 1968 Act was never used.

Attempts have been made to involve the Parliamentary Ombudsman (Commissioner for Administration) who is responsible for investigating complaints referred to him by members of the House of Commons where members of the public claim to have suffered injustice by reason of action taken by Government Departments. A member of the public complained that the Minister responsible had not used his powers to direct Avon to build sites and therefore the complainant was suffering from unauthorised caravans in a neighbouring road. The Commissioner ruled that insufficient time had elapsed since the County of Avon had been formed, after reorganisation of local government in 1974, for them to have been able to form a policy and develop sites. A direction has now been given to Avon to provide more pitches.

Complaints to the Local Government Commissioner have been more successful. Hackney and Tower Hamlets were found guilty of maladministration in not providing a site. Both councils have now done so. In 1984 Staffordshire County Council was criticised for 'taking ten years to get nowhere' in the provision of a site in the Lyme valley. No compensation has ever been awarded to Gypsies but a house-dweller was more lucky. In 1988 the Local Government

Ombudsman ruled that Sevenoaks Council was guilty in not removing some Gypsies from land neighbouring the complainant, land which they owned themselves and had been living on (although without planning permission) from before the house-dweller had bought her house. She was awarded compensation.

The Public Order Act of 1986

One of the provisions of the Public Order Act increases pressure on unsited Gypsies, although it was introduced to deal with New Age Travellers. We deal elsewhere with other parts of the Act which concern incitement to racial hatred.

As a result of the confrontations between New Age Travellers and police in 1986 the Government decided to introduce new measures against trespass in the Public Order Bill during its passage through the House of Lords. The new clause was tabled on 26th September 1986. Four days later the Department of the Environment wrote to interested organisations 'consulting' them about the clause. They had less than a week to reply before the debate took place. The replies we have seen all protested but it was in vain.The new clause was added to the Bill.

Under the new provisions (Section 39 of the Act) a police officer can order trespassers to leave land without a court order if:

> "(a) any of those persons has caused damage to property on the land or used threatening, abusive or insulting words or behaviour ... or (b) have between them brought twelve or more vehicles on to the land."

If they don't leave any uniformed policeman can arrest them without a warrant.

Gerald Kaufman, spokesman for the Opposition, raised the question of Gypsies.

> "Gypsies had better travel in small groups. As long as they travel with twelve caravans or fewer and behave themselves they will be all right. The moment they travel

in groups of twelve or more, they will be in trouble."
Douglas Hogg, for the Government, replied:

"The right honourable gentleman (Mr Kaufman) belly-
ached about Gypsies. The purpose of the new clause is not
to harass innocent Gypsies. However, if Gypsies create the
nuisance contemplated by the Bill, I see no reason why it
should not be extended to cover them."

In fact, Gypsies had to travel in groups of less than six
families as a caravan and a lorry count as two vehicles.
The Home Office wrote in February 1987.

"Neither the Government or the police have any wish to
harass well-behaved Travellers ... Highways were
specifically excluded from the scope of the section so that
Gypsies can stop on them."

So Gypsy families were encouraged by this law to stop on the
edge of roads, with all the inherent dangers, rather than pull
into a piece of unoccupied land.
This new legislation was soon in force. In April 1987 two
families of Travellers parked on a piece of park land in
Haringey. Because they had 'damaged' the surrounding fence
when they took it down in order to get into the park, they
came within the rules of the new Act. John W. as well as his
wife, and Mrs M. in the second caravan were all three fined
£40 and £10 costs.
The new Criminal Justice and Public Order Act (see
below) tightens up the provisions on trespass.

New Age Travellers
'New Age Travellers' is a term used for individuals or families
who have recently taken to the road. We shall restrict
ourselves to looking at whether New Age Travellers are
classed as Gypsies for the purposes of the Caravan Sites Act.
That is to say, did local authorities have any obligation under
this Act to provide them with sites? And can New Age
Travellers claim any special consideration if they apply for a

private caravan site?

The operative wording in the Act is 'of nomadic habit of life' and the first question is how long someone has to be on the road to be so defined. In 1986 a Yorkshire court ruled that a group known as 'The Mutants' were Gypsies within the meaning of the Act. In Avon a New Age Traveller, Mr Rexworthy, was ruled to be a Gypsy. On the other hand a court in Berkshire ruled that a Ms B. had not proved "her intent to be a Gypsy".

In recent years the Government has stated in correspondence with advice agencies and in Parliament that it does not on the whole see the New Age Travellers as Gypsies, to be helped by the 1968 Act.

The recent decision on appeal in the case of South Hams District Council v. Gibb has ruled that 'nomadism' means travelling with an economic purpose. Anyone who moves merely because the police move them is not a nomad, nor is someone who travels from place to place for pleasure. Romany Gypsies living on a caravan site who travel only to visit fairs to see friends and relatives lose their status as 'Gypsies' under the 1968 Act. On the other hand New Age Travellers who travel either to work or to seek work may acquire the status of 'Gypsies'.

The General Elections of 1987 and 1991
In the run up to the 1987 General Election Conservative candidates in particular used the Gypsy issue to win votes. Christopher Murphy, MP Welwyn-Hatfield, brought in a short bill entitled Gypsies (Control of Unauthorised Encampments) Act 1987 which would have designated the whole of England and Wales as an area where Gypsies could not stop and made outlaws at a stroke of some 4,000 families.

In March 1987 Peter Lilley (MP for St Albans) initiated a debate on Gypsy Caravan Sites. He wanted no more sites to be built in either Green Belt or residential areas as, he said, the majority of the public do not want to live "cheek by jowl" with Gypsies. His suggestion was to put sites in out of the way rural areas. He talked too of an influx of a previously unheard of group called "Irish didicois" who should not be classed as Gypsies and for whom no sites should be provided. Another MP, Sir Hugh Rossi, claimed in the debate that his constituents "suffered horrendous problems because of an invasion of the area by so-called Gypsies." Seven years later these suggestions were incorporated in legislation.

During the 1987 election Conservative Party officials in Bradford were seen handing out stickers for cars bearing the message: "Keep the Gypsies out – Vote Conservative". After protests the stickers were withdrawn.

It should be said that at local level there has been little difference between Labour and Conservative councillors in their attitude to providing sites for Gypsies. In Hackney Labour man David Pollock lists (in his leaflet) achievements by De Beauvoir's remaining two Labour councillors to back his party's case. He said "Councillors Michael Barber and Carole Young ... have ensured the eviction of travellers."

The new Government elected in 1987 had a fresh report compiled by Professor Wibberley. Its recommendations were not dissimilar to those of John Cripps. Published in 1986 they are still valid and we give below the most important.

■ The definition of a Gypsy should be made a little more specific.

■ Better and more frequent counts on the numbers are needed.

■ Equity and efficiency of designation can be improved by reviews of areas now designated, the withdrawal of designation orders in bad cases and stronger pressure on recalcitrant authorities.

■ There must be a speeding up of the process of providing authorised local authority sites and a concerted attempt to increase the range and number of private sites.

■ There is a need for some provision of transit sites, primarily long distance travellers.

There was little action by the Government elected in 1987. In view of the anti-Gypsy views expressed by many Government MPs during the General Election campaign, Gypsies may well have breathed a sigh of relief as any legislation might well have worsened their situation.

Nicholas Ridley summed up the situation in a Parliamentary Reply in February 1987:

"The Government has decided that there should be no amendment of the legislation at this stage."

And falling back on the need for more information, as had his predecessor in 1950:

"An early priority will be to examine how information on Gypsy numbers could be improved."

The Gypsy Sites Branch of the Department was to get a sixth member, attached to the Social Research Division, who would carry out a research programme and supervise privatised research contracts.

By the time of the 1991 General Election New Age Travellers were high on the agenda. In his speech to the Conservative Conference before the election Mr Major highlighted the need to control New Age Travellers and for more toilets on the motorways as priorities for the new government.

This time there was to be action as we show below.

The 1994 Criminal Justice and Public Order Act

The first step after the 1991 Election was the issuing of a joint press release by the Home Office and the Department of the Environment announcing the intention to reform the 1968 Caravan Sites Act. A consultation document was then issued and over a thousand replies were received, mostly opposing the idea of repealing the 1968 Caravan Sites Act. The Government pressed ahead however and – in spite of the opposition of the Labour and Liberal Democrats in the House of Commons and all-party opposition in the House of Lords – new measures were enacted as part of the 1994 Criminal Justice and Public Order Act.

The number of vehicles needed to commit criminal trespass was reduced to six, which means that a maximum of two families (two caravans and two towing vehicles) can stop together on roadside sites. The powers given by 'designation' under the 1968 Act to councils that had provided enough sites were made nationwide. Not moving within a reasonable time after being asked to do so by a local council becomes a further criminal offence. A new government circular will ask councils to tolerate unauthorised sites where these 'cause no nuisance'. (Tolerated sites in this sense should be distinguished from the toleration of private sites which do not have planning permission).

The greatest blow for Gypsies in the new Act is the repeal of the 1968 Caravan Sites Act. This does not just mean that councils no longer need to build sites. It means that they can close the sites they have already built and, with the disappearance of the duty on councils to provide sites, the absence of a pitch will be of less weight in a defence against an accusation of trespass or an application for planning permission for a private site.

Private sites
After 1945 a number of Gypsies bought plots of land mainly to use as a winter base. However, a Caravan Sites Act in 1960 was followed by three Town and Country Planning Acts which made it almost impossible for individual Gypsies any longer to get planning permission to site one caravan or for larger landowners, Gypsy or Gorgio, to build caravan sites.

Sites opened after 1960 without planning permission were closed by enforcement orders. In 1970 Dorking closed the site at the Journey's End Cafe, Sevenoaks required the 'discontinuance' of the Three Ways site, the then Hollingbourn Rural District Council used the 1962 Planning Act against two families on a caravan site called 'Leytonstone'.

The list is lengthy. Hundreds of families have been turned off their own land or other privately owned sites which did not have planning permission. Sites bought before 1960 which do not need planning permission because they had 'established use' have been refused site licences. This meant only the owners of the land can stop on them or they were taken over by councils and closed using Compulsory Purchase Order.

Greenbanks in Walton-on-Thames housed ninety caravans, mainly Gypsies. After the land had been purchased the Council built houses while the Gypsies were driven out of the area, as far as London. In 1971 Epsom took over Cox's Lane site, ran it for a while, and then turned the residents off. Some years later they had to reopen it as an official Gypsy site and let many of the original inhabitants on again. The unfortunate families from Cox's Lane had spent many years on the roadside because of this act of bureaucratic folly.

Local authorities just did not like the idea of large numbers of Gypsy families living freely in their area. The picturesque Greenwich site was taken over, its leafy alleyways removed and a concrete field built, a design which won an architectural prize. Whenever a Council took over a site it reduced the number of families provided for and these too went to join the thousands on the road.

Enforcement action against privately owned sites was condemned by central government.

"Where local authorities are considering the timing of planning enforcement action against travelling families who may have bought a plot of land and have stationed their caravan on it without the necessary planning permission and site licence, in some circumstances it may be possible to defer enforcement action until sites have been established in the county to which such families could go." (Circular MHLG 38/70)

In spite of this, local councils issued and still issue ' enforcement orders'. One example from many was Chelmsford Council's action against Mr and Mrs M. in 1988. Even though there were no sites in the district they tried to force this family off their own land, justifying their action by the danger of 'ribbon development' along the road.

In 1977 the Government, following the Cripps Report, asked for a more sympathetic attitude in looking at planning applications.

"In view of the urgent need for more sites, local authorities may wish to consider the advantages of encouraging (Gypsy owned sites). It may involve a sympathetic and flexible approach to applications for *planning permission* and site licences." (Circular DoE 28/77)

This paragraph is still valid.

This too has been ignored. 90 per cent of all applications are refused and have to go to appeal. In December 1987 Mr T. was refused permission by Epping Forest District Council.

"The proposal is contrary to Policy 36 of the Draft Local Plan which states that Planning Permission will not be granted for use of land as a Gypsy caravan site within the Local Plan Area." (Planning Application EPF/1490/87)

On appeal Gypsies often face a Catch 22 situation. Although they are supposed to be given special consideration, it has been argued by councils that the applicants, because they have bought land, are no longer of nomadic habit of life, so no longer Gypsies and, therefore, do not merit special consideration. This argument was accepted by the Department of the Environment Inspector in 1975.

"Turning to the submission that your client is a Gypsy who wishes a permanent home for himself, his wife and six children and should accordingly be treated as a special case, it was indicated to me that Mr F's real desire was to build a bungalow on the appeal site and the proposed caravan developments before me under appeal were somewhat inadequate alternatives. While this motive is commendable it appears to indicate, when coupled with the fact that Mr F. and his family have lived on the appeal site for five years, that he has given up his nomadic habit of life. I accordingly see no reason to disagree with the Magistrates' Court decision in 1972 that Mr F. was not a Gypsy in terms of Section 16 of the Caravan Sites Act." (Appeal T/APP/2081/A/73/442,444,443(G5))

Forced off his own land by this decision, Mr F. then had to wander the country before he again became legally a Gypsy.

Although in one similar case recently the Secretary of State overturned an Inspector's decision that a Gypsy who had settled down was no longer a Gypsy as defined by the 1968 Act, this view has not always been shared by the courts.

Even if they are accepted as Gypsies they may not always benefit if the Inspector is unaware of or ignores Government policy. In Essex in 1980, in spite of earlier circulars, Mr A. the Inspector was "not aware that Gypsies should be treated differently from other applicants." (T/APP/5217/A/79/09422)

At the time the first edition of this pamphlet was published fifteen families, including twenty seven children, had recently been evicted from their homes in the Runnymede district of Surrey and a few miles away, another sixteen families faced the same bleak fate in Waverley district. The Secretary of State for the Environment refused planning permission on appeal for both these groups. Since then there have been further evictions from private sites in Surrey at Smithers Rough and elsewhere.

In January 1994 the Department of the Environment issued a circular which said that private Gypsy sites should normally no longer be in Green Belt or other land with a protected status, such as Special Landscape Areas. This has made it more difficult to get permission for sites, at the same time as the Government has proclaimed as a policy that Gypsies should provide their own caravan sites.

Who is a Gypsy ?

Although for the purposes of the Race Relations Act Gypsies are an ethnic group, for the 1968 Caravan Sites Act they were a social group, "persons of nomadic habit of life". Lord Bridges in the case of Greenwich LBC v. Powell (House of Lords Nov./Dec.1988) suggested that seasonal nomadism was necessary to retain a nomadic habit of life and Gypsy status. (It was argued that some of the tenants on the Greenwich Gypsy site were still legally Gypsies even though they only travelled in the summer. This meant that the site was still a

Gypsy site and the Council could evict tenants without a court order, whether the family were Gypsies or not.)

This guidance was followed by the High Court in a case involving an appeal against the refusal of planning permission – Horsham DC v. Secretary of State for the Environment and Mark Giles (13 Oct 1989). They overruled the decision of an inspector that Mr Giles was a Gypsy and said that, although he was of Romany origin, he no longer had Gypsy status because he had stopped travelling. He was not therefore entitled to special consideration in his planning application for a private site.

This judgment has been refined by the further ruling in the case of South Hams v. Gibb (1994). The judges said that not only must there be at least seasonal nomadism, but the nomadism must be for an economic purpose. Wandering aimlessly around the countryside is not nomadism.

At many enquiries where Gypsies are trying to get permission to station a caravan on their own land much time is spent debating whether the applicant has lost his Gypsy status. It comes as a surprise to the applicant that, even though all his life he has been treated as a Gypsy both by his family and the authorities, he is no longer legally one when it comes to trying to get sympathetic consideration for trying to find a place to legally stop.

Discrimination

Gypsies have suffered discrimination by being refused service in public houses and shops, entry to dance halls and youth clubs, even on at least one occasion (in Sheffield) not allowed on a bus.

Discrimination is not a new phenomenon. Here is an example taken from an article in *The Countryman* recalling the 1920s.

> "In season, the itinerants poured in, to pea pick, single out and so on; tramps, Gypsies and Travellers of every kind. 'No Gypos' read the notice on the pub door."

The Commission for Racial Equality and its predecessor, the Race Relations Board, received many complaints in particular about pubs with 'No Gypsies' signs outside. Letters 'achieved some success' in the removal of signs but recently new wording 'No Travellers' has been used. Under the Race Relations Act such a sign may be seen as discriminating *indirectly* against Romany Gypsies. The pub owner would need to justify the sign and a suitable test case is awaited to see how these notices could be justified. Under the Race Relations Act only the CRE can prosecute a discriminator. All that Gypsies can do is refer these signs, and refusals of service, to the CRE and leave it to the Commission to decide which cases to take up.

Notices are becoming more subtle, such as 'Travellers by Appointment only', so that a Gypsy with limited reading ability will see the sign as applying to him, but in case of prosecution the landlord might get away with arguing that he was referring to commercial travellers.

In two cases where clubs rather than pubs were concerned, the cases were settled out of court with an apology to the Traveller who had been refused entry. One involved an Irish Traveller but – because it never reached the stage of a trial – the argument that Irish Travellers are an ethnic group has never been settled.

One of the few cases where Race Relations legislation was pursued to a conclusion was in the village of Brymbo in Wales. Gypsy family J. lived in a caravan in a gravel pit in this village. Both parents had been born in nearby villages and had lived in the area all their lives. They had ten children. In 1978 they registered on the housing waiting list and in 1980 a house became vacant and it was expected that it would be offered to the family.

A local house dweller Mrs S. organised a petition headed: "We the signatories of the attached petition wish to state that we object strongly to the housing of a further Gypsy family in Brynbo". Over 300 local residents signed the petition. Mrs S. was reported in a local paper as saying that there was already one Gypsy family in the vicinity and that she thought that the district where this empty house was situated was likely to become "a Gypsy site". She was further reported as saying that "the Gypsies will move in here over our dead bodies".

In May 1981 the CRE ruled that Mrs S., a Mrs G. and the Brymbo Community Council had "attempted to induce Wrexham and Maelor Borough Council to discriminate unlawfully in the disposal of council housing in contravention of the Race Relations Act". They were ordered to stop their campaign.

Discrimination in the field of employment has been widely reported. Recent cases from Kent include a male

Traveller who was turned down for work as a night watchman when he gave as his address the local caravan site. A young woman from the same site was also rejected for factory work, with the added problem that because of her age she was also being refused Income Support.

Police – "Gypsies are trouble"

The police attitude towards Gypsies is ambivalent. On the one hand they may be friendly, especially in country districts where police are recruited locally, with individuals whose families they will have known since childhood. On the other hand, they have to stand by 'to prevent a breach of the peace' i.e. assist council officials or court bailiffs to evict Gypsies. And they know, even if the council and magistrates don't, that when they move them on the caravans will not disappear but turn up again somewhere else and the whole process will have to start again. As one policeman said to a meeting of teachers and other workers with Gypsies:

> "Gypsies are trouble. If I move them on, I get you people or the local vicar complaining about persecution and harassment – if I don't move them on, then the people in the houses complain to my sergeant that I haven't done my duty."

In many areas a police force may have a Gypsy Liaison Officer or the Community Liaison Officer is in regular contact with local Gypsy spokesmen. But harassment is still common.

Gypsies on unofficial sites see a police car draw up at five in the morning, hear the bang on the caravan window with a baton. Police may confiscate the water churn 'for checking' although they rarely nowadays find a cooking pot to tip into the fire (as recounted to Norman Dodds).

All the following incidents are from reports by Gypsy organisations.

> "In March 1966 Mr D. a housed-welling Traveller known as a Civil Rights activist and his brother were walking home from a fish and chip shop. Two policemen on

motorbikes came up to them, accused them of 'whistling at a policeman' and asked for their names. The police then abused them for being Gypsies and pulled out their truncheons. Mr D. was handcuffed and kicked several times. He was then arrested and charged with assault. His mother, who had been watching TV in their house all the evening, ran out from the house when she heard the noise. She was arrested and charged with being drunk and disorderly."

In court all the charges were dismissed.

A common complaint is the over-reaction in the case of minor problems.

"A policeman outside a site in East London saw a woman swerving her car. He thought she was drunk, though in fact she was trying to avoid a pothole in the road. She indignantly refused to take a breath test and the police officer then called for help on his radio. Thirty policemen in squad cars arrived. The woman's husband came out to argue with the police as did other relatives and neighbours. Seven persons were arrested and taken to the police station. They were released except for one who decided to plead guilty to assaulting the police."

"In an East Anglian town in 1987 a house-dweller reported to the police that he thought a young child from the neighbouring official caravan site had stolen his son's bicycle. A busload of police turned up to arrest an eleven year old boy. In the event no charges were laid."

A dispute between neighbours can lead to mass intervention:

"Armed police surrounded a Gypsy site for more than five hours after a family feud. More than fifty police including a firearms unit moved in to seal off the camp. The dawn raid was carried out simultaneously with another raid as more than 100 police swooped on a second site in the area."

"In 1988 150 police came to Outwood, in Surrey, to 'look for two stolen cars'. They then took a great deal of property from the caravans. Later the same day a child threw a stone at a police car. Fifty police in riot gear then rushed onto the site and 'did it over' ".

In the same month police descended on a site in Sussex and arrested all the men who were held for two months without bail. The worst incident perhaps has been in the county of Bedfordshire where police carried out a 'mock raid' with machine guns (sic) on a roadside camp as a demonstration for visiting continental officers.

In Sheffield there are a few officers whom the Gypsies have nicknamed 'The Gypsy Squad'.

"They come on to the sites at two or three in the morning with blue lights flashing on their cars and just sit in their cars on the site. On one occasion they came with a warrant for a thirty year old man and because they couldn't find they took away a seventeen year old on the same warrant."

Under the Criminal Evidence Act police can arrest anyone and hold them for forty eight hours. *City Limits* reported that under-age children were being held in police stations under this law. While researching this pamphlet we were told, and have no reason to doubt this, that Irish and English Travellers have been threatened with arrest under the Prevention of Terrorism Act unless they move off an unauthorised stopping place.

Social Security

Traditionally, Gypsies did not ask the State for help at any stage of their lives. Born with an aunt acting as midwife, looking after their own handicapped children, supporting relatives and friends when money was short, having a 'whip round' for cash to replace someone's burnt out caravan and supporting their aged parents in a bungalow. But times have changed. Families and friends can no longer stay together because of site regulations and the disappearance of the larger traditional stopping places. Craft work is hard to sell and with several million unemployed there is less call for the odd job man, as the out of work and poor do their own repairs and gardening and keep their cars and refrigerators until they are too old for resale, except as scrap metal.

Farm labour has been replaced by machines or Gorgio women are bussed in from neighbouring towns. Daily horoscopes in the paper are cheaper than the palm reader. A breadwinner may have a spell in prison because of some technical motoring offence while rules on official sites prevent any work being done near the caravan.

There is, therefore, poverty in many sections of the Travelling community and Gypsies – for the first time – have to turn to Social Services for support and to Social Security for cash. But this is not easy.

"There seems to be an inconsistency of treatment to the Travellers compared with anybody else claiming. A typical example is that most people would be required to sign on once every two weeks in order to get benefit whereas with Travellers here the DHSS expect them to sign on every day. They won't give them travelling expenses for that and the only way to do it is to walk or take a cut in food money to pay for the bus."

And again from the same area (Port Talbot):

"In some areas, DHSS offices will pay with one form of identification, whereas in this particular area you won't be paid without two. We had one case of a woman with five children who had to wait two or three weeks before she received any money from the DHSS. She survived on charity parcels from the Salvation Army and the Church Army."

Circular S50 issued in 1985, 'Verification of Identity – Preventing Fraud', caused problems for many Gypsies. This circular instructed DHSS offices not to accept baptismal certificates as a means of identity. They should ask for full birth certificates or driving licences. This particularly hit Irish Travellers whose birth was often not registered and, of course, not all women hold driving licences.

"At the end of 1987 the S. family had all their documents taken away, suspected of being forgeries. While waiting for their return they had to move to another town where the local Travellers Support Group assisted them in obtaining duplicate birth and marriage certificates."

The North London Regional Fraud Office designed its own 'Itinerant Caravan Dwellers Information Card'. This asked DHSS officers to record 'physical features, skin colour, known associates and criminal record'. This card was withdrawn after pressure from a Citizens Advice Bureau. However, in 1986 the DHSS convened the 'Nomadic Claimants Working Party' mainly to deal with New Age Travellers. In 1986 this Working Party reported and suggested setting up a regional index. The form from which we print extracts below appears to be the one used for this index.

NOMADIC CLAIMANT
The following claim has been made.
1   Name
6   Identity confirmed: Yes or No.
     If Yes, state means of Identity accepted.
7   Description and other distinguishing features.
     Known by any other names (give details)

The form was to go to the Supplementary Benefit Section Regional Office in Gabalfa. Item 7 seems to imply that a nomadic claimant is likely to be simultaneously claiming at more than one office. Yet anyone with experience of a DSS office will know that claiming is a full-time job in one place let alone two different offices (in spite of the occasional case that hits the headlines).

The new Social Fund, which replaces Special Needs Payments, is unlikely to make payments, which are normally repayable loans, to any of the over 3,000 Gypsy families with no fixed address. Sixteen and seventeen year olds are having difficulties in complying with the new rules for benefit, under which they have to get on a training course and find an employer who will take them as a trainee. This is difficult enough for a Gypsy on a caravan site and impossible for the nomad.

Health

It is clear from a number of reports that the travelling life today is not particularly healthy. As Dr Heller, a GP, and Beryl Peck, a Health Visitor, reported in Sheffield:

"The problems caused by poor sanitation, inadequate water supply and poverty, as well as the stress and fear that Gypsy families live under, cause a variety of problems we would be more familiar with in less developed (sic) countries."

They list a number of conditions directly attributable to the adverse conditions in which the Gypsies had lived their lives, mainly on illegal sites: "uncorrected squints, unrecognized deafness, eczema, untreated cuts and burns, tetanus, bronchitis, etc."

A research worker from the London School of Hygiene found in Sheffield that in 1981 a high percentage of all pregnancies ended in perinatal death (before the child was one month old). The report quotes the example of Mrs C. who: "had to leave hospital the day after her child was stillborn. Fear of eviction made her rush back to her caravan. What chance wound infection".

A survey carried out in Kent by Dr Vaile and Ms Pahl of the Health Services Research Unit in Canterbury found for example that 35 per cent of all families had no means of receiving post which, as the authors point out, means that letters from clinics or hospitals do not reach the people to whom they are sent. Infant mortality figures were again higher than national and regional averages. The survey found that the places where Gypsies lived were "areas which would not normally be used for residential development, such as an old rubbish tip, a site adjoining a motorway, a sewage plant or a busy railway line".

Many nomadic Gypsies find it difficult to get treatment from a GP, although under the Terms of Service of a General Medical Practitioner (Regulation 19) doctors who refuses to take a person on to their list must still provide 'immediate necessary treatment' for up to fourteen days. In one documented case, a doctor in Wiltshire refused to treat a Gypsy woman and her daughter. The mother needed a further supply of penicillin and the daughter a letter of referral to a hospital.

Most families prefer to go to a casualty department where they will normally be accepted for treatment without discrimination. Some experts think the new regulations for medical practices which came into force in April 1990 will not help Gypsies to get treatment. For example, doctors may be reluctant to start a series of injections with a Gypsy child if they think that the family will move on before the full series is completed. This would make it harder for the practice to reach the necessary percentage of children with completed injections for payment to be made, so they will lose funds. So far there is no evidence of this happening.

Education

This section is based partly on a report prepared by Thomas Acton, Gian Douglas-Home and Donald Kenrick for the European Commission.

After the English Education Act of 1902 extended compulsory schooling to the whole population, there was a need to regularise the position of Gypsies. This was done in the Children's Acts of 1908 by which children of nomadic parents were required to attend for only 200 half-days (instead of the normal 400). This provision was rarely enforced and few children attended school.

After the founding of the Gypsy Council in 1966 the first caravan school in Britain was run by volunteers in the summer of the following year. Following this, a number of short-lived 'Romano Drom' (Romany Road) schools were started in England and Wales. In 1967 too, the Ministry of Education published the Plowden Report *Children and their Schools* which described Gypsy children as 'probably the most deprived group in the country'.

In 1968 the NGEC (National Gypsy Education Council) was set up with a committee of Gypsy activists and educationalists. Lady Plowden (chair of the committee which produced the report) was invited to head this new body and the NGEC with its respectable image was able to gain more grants from charitable funds than had the Gypsy Council's own education committee. An independent voluntary project was set up in the Midlands which continued' till 1976. Overlapping this was the Joint Service for Travelling Children created by eleven local education authorities in the West Midlands. Over the years voluntary schemes have gradually been replaced by LEA provision.

In 1973 the Department of Education and Science ran the first official course on the Education of Travelling Children, organised by Donald Buckland HMI and Chris Reiss. Twenty three teachers attended. This course was repeated every year until 1976 when, as part of government cuts, it was changed to be held every two years. In 1988 the course took place in Nottingham and drew over 100 participants. These courses have now been cut completely. In the same year as the Nottingham course the NGEC split and there were then two organisations, the NGEC and ACERT (The Advisory Council for the Education of Romanies and Other Travellers), both engaged in furthering the cause of Gypsy education. The NGEC recently recognised its wider brief by changing its name to the Gypsy Council for Education, Culture, Welfare and Civil Rights.

In 1977 Croydon's Education Committee caused a furore when in a test case it refused to admit a certain Mary Delaney to its schools on the ground that she was on an illegal site. Joint protests by NGEC and ACERT, together with a threat to take the British Government to the European Court, persuaded the Government to insert a clause in the 1980 Education Act to block the loophole by which Croydon might legally have been able to exclude children from illegal sites.

Circular 1/81 of the Department of Education and Science declared explicitly the right of Gypsy children to attend school.

"The reference to children 'in the area' of the authority means that each authority's duty extends to all children residing in their area, whether permanently or temporarily. The duty thus embraces in particular travelling children, including Gypsies."

Most Gypsy parents, in theory at least, welcome the chance of primary education for their children. However, as their children reach puberty and the subjects on offer seem less relevant to real life (life within their community and earning one's living), attitudes change. Research has shown that as the children get older, attendance drops off. Perhaps a third of all Gypsy children are attending school regularly, the majority of primary age. Parents, worried that their offspring will learn to take drugs, swear and hear about sex from young house-dwellers, do not discourage their older daughters from staying at home or their sons from going out with other male Gypsies to learn about work at first hand. It is likely that only the possibility of attending single sex schools and a curriculum orientated to practical activities will encourage a greater attendance by 11-16 year olds.

The Government has taken a moderate role in all this. In 1983 they published an HMI Discussion Paper *The Education of Travellers' Children* giving some case histories of good educational practice. A further help has been the establishment of a new fund to which local authorities can apply for educational work with Gypsy children or adults. Money from this fund has been available from 1st April 1990 but because a fixed sum has been allocated nationally many projects have been turned down or given less than requested.

Within schools, prejudice against Gypsies continues in many subtle and unsubtle ways. Children told the researchers during the EC project that they had been left to draw at the back of the class, of exclusion from Christmas Parties, even of not getting commemorative spoons on the occasion of Prince Charles' marriage.

The report details how a house-dwelling Gypsy child went to school for less than a week at the age of five. He was rebuked by a teacher for putting some chalk in his pocket and never went back to school. Four years, and three educational social workers later, home tuition was arranged for the boy.

The Swann report (*Education for All*) had a section on *The Educational Needs of Travellers' Children*. It talks of the "extreme hostility" which the travelling community faces from the settled community:

> "The degree of hostility towards Gypsies' and other Travellers' children if they do enter school is quite remarkable even when set alongside the racism encountered by children from other ethnic minority groups."

A survey in Sheffield found that 'racist name calling' was what the Traveller children most hated about going to school. In 1994, in a school in the Greater London area, Gypsy children were subjected to name calling and attacks. Gorgio children blocked the school gate and prevented them leaving school and going home until the police were called. On another occasion the provoked Gypsy children retaliated. Three Gypsy children were suspended but no Gorgio children were punished.

In conclusion we must agree with Hegerty. In a follow up to the Swann Report, twenty-one years after the Plowden report found Gypsies to be probably the most severely deprived children educationally in the country, he wrote: "It is clear that there has been a substantial failure to meet the needs of Gypsy children".

The Gypsy Council and the fight for sites

Norman Dodds and his Gypsy friends (see section 13 above) were not alone in their struggle. In Dorset Romany activist Tom Jonell was active from 1963 to 1968, while in 1963 too Tom O'Doherty, an Irish Traveller, founded the Society of Travelling People in Leeds.

Two years later, Richard Hauser of the Centre for Group Studies and his wife, the pianist Hephzibah Menuhin, hosted a meeting which was the first step in changing the face of the Gypsy political scene. Those present included Vaida Voevod of the Communauté Mondiale Gitane (see below), David Smith (author of several reports on Gypsies) and Brian Richardson, active in the National Council for Civil Liberties. Then in 1966 Grattan Puxon (a journalist who had been drawn into the fight for Travellers' Rights in Ireland) returned to England. He drew together Gypsies and their Gorgio supporters who later that same year took a lead in setting up the Gypsy Council. An impressive list of thirty Gypsies were on the leaflet calling all Travellers to come to a meeeting in Kent on 11th December 1966 to support the following demands:

1 camping sites
2 equal rights to education,work and houses

3 equal standing through respect between ourselves and our settled neighbours.

An additional twist was that the venue, the Bull's Head, was a public house which had a 'No Gypsies' sign on the front, a fact which the press made much of. The new Gypsy Council was to thrive on media publicity.

Over the next few years Puxon and other leaders of the Council and their Gorgio supporters were to run a campaign of passive resistance to evictions of caravans which hit the press and TV screen. Puxon himself drew inspiration from Gandhi's 'passive resistance' and the movement to drive the British out of India, while experience of CND and the anti-Vietnam demonstrations either in person or as a TV viewer was common to all.

People from all walks of life supported the campaign for stopping places and education. Links were forged between Gypsies and Gorgios and a 'bust card' was printed which at its peak had twenty three phone numbers across England, Wales and Scotland. At the first sign of a bailiff a Gypsy would run to the nearest public telephone and a mixture of housewives, duffle-coated pastors and others would assemble with the Gypsies making a human barrier between their caravans and the council officials with their accompanying police and towing vehicles. This campaign was a major factor in persuading the Government to take some action over the 'Gypsy problem', culminating in the 1968 Caravan Sites Act

The battle for sites wound down during the 1970s for a number of reasons. Many of the most obstinate local councils opened sites, splits within the Gypsy Council weakened its leadership and the fact that caravans were becoming more expensive meant that their owners were no longer willing to risk damage during an eviction but were inclined to move off at the first sight of bailiffs. It will be interesting to see whether Gypsies meekly accept the new law on criminal trespass or whether the lack of alternative stopping places leads to a new campaign of resistance.

Realignments within the Gypsy civil rights movement led to the formation of the Romany Guild in 1972, the

National Gypsy Council in 1974 and in 1975 the Association of Gypsy Organisations, the latter no longer operating as an independent organisation (having merged with the renamed NGEC). At the time of writing there are also other groups with regional rather than national membership. We list the major organisations in an appendix.

The international movement

In 1959 Ionel Rotaru, using the old chieftain's title, Vaida Voevod, emerged in Paris as would-be leader of the world's Gypsies. He founded an international organisation Communauté Mondiale Gitane (CMG). This was banned by the French Government in 1965 but Vanko Rouda and other ex-members of the CMG formed a new organisation, the Comité International Tzigane (CIT). As they did not register it officially the French Government has not been able to dissolve it. Grattan Puxon and the Dublin-based Itinerant Action Group were in contact with both the CMG and the CIT, and Vanko Rouda spoke at the foundation meeting of the Gypsy Council.

In 1971 the Gypsy Council was host to the First World Romany Congress. The CIT, now called the Comité International Rom, was active in mustering support for this meeting which was attended by delegates and observers from over fourteen countries. From the Congress emerged a flag (blue and green with a red wheel), an anthem and five commissions which were to meet between congresses.

The second Congress was held in Geneva in 1978 with 120 delegates and observers from twenty six countries. The link with India was a predominant theme of this congress which opened with the presentation by W. R. Rishi from Chandigarh of a symbolic package of earth from the historical mother country of the Romanies. New statutes were elaborated and a new organisation emerged, the Romany Union, which was to operate between congresses and which in the following year gained recognition from UNESCO.

The Third Congress was held in Gottingen, Germany, in 1981 with even larger numbers, some 300 delegates and observers. Prominence was given to recalling the Nazi period.

Invited Jewish speakers included Simon Wiesenthal and Richard Hauser. A new demand was made for global reparations from the German government. This has not yet been met but Bonn does now support the national German Gypsy Union based in Heidelberg. An international praesidium or committee was elected with Peter Mercer as the British member.

As frontiers of Eastern Europe began to open up the Fourth Congress was held near Warsaw in Poland. Over 300 persons from twenty countries attended including important delegations from the Soviet Union, Romania, Czechoslovakia and Bulgaria. Amongst the decisions were the setting up of commissions to produce a standard Romani literary language and an encyclopaedia. There was a reaffirmation of the Indian origin of the Romanies while recognising that they would remain citizens of the countries where they now live. The British and Irish delegations stressed the need for caravan sites and education.

The Romany Union is taking part in setting up a new overall international body on which all Gypsy organisations will be represented and which will work in particular with the Commission for Security and Co-operation in Europe set up by the great powers in Helsinki.

European organisations
Council of Europe
The Council of Europe covers over thirty countries. It has no powers over its members and has until now had a low profile in countries such as Britain which have joined the European Community.

Nevertheless it played a part in raising consciousness of the Gypsy issue at international level. As early as 1969 the Consultative Assembly made a recommendation that member states should try and improve the conditions of life of their Gypsy citizens.

The Committee of Ministers of the Council, noting that nothing had been done as a result of the above mentioned recommendation, in 1975 passed a strongly worded resolution. This called for an end to discrimination, the safeguarding of the culture of *nomadic populations*, the building of caravan sites and encouraging the education of children and adults.

In 1981 the Conference of Local and Regional Authorities noted that the situation of nomads, especially Gypsies, had not improved since 1969 and recommended the Committee of Ministers to study the possibility of setting up a fund to finance cultural and general help for nomads and to organise a system of identity cards enabling Travellers to move from country to country. There were other recommendations but these two would have been very useful if they had been acted upon.

The Parliamentary Assembly of the Council of Europe proposed a number of measures in its Recommendation 1203 of 1993. These covered a range of issues from culture to civil rights but the Council has no power to enforce these proposals.

The Council of Europe financed and published a most useful survey on Gypsies in all the member states, *Gypsies and Travellers*, of which a second edition has come out this year. Meetings for teachers and others involved in education have been held in Donaueschingen and elsewhere and reports of the discussions and conclusions have been circulated. Finally, it has initiated a project for the history of minorities, including Gypsies, to be included in the history textbooks and teaching programmes of member state.

The European Union
As early as 1981 members of the World Romany Union first approached the European Community (as it was then called). There was a delay until 1984 when the European Parliament decided to study school provision. Information was collected from all member countries and published in 1986.

At the end of the study there are forty three recommendations. They are farsighted and include:

"That teaching material incorporating elements of Gypsy and Traveller culture, language and history be developed."
"That Travellers be employed in connection with the schooling of their children."

Needs other than education were not forgotten: "Nomadism must be officially recognised and provision made for nomads."

The study was accepted by the Education Committee and has been published in many of the Community languages. Since then, a number of meetings of teachers and educationalists, as well as representatives of the Gypsies, have been held, and the study has been enlarged to cover Spain and Portugal. Gypsies await further positive action in the form of pressure on governments to provide a framework within which their children can receive education, as well as finance for adult training programmes. This may come from a resolution of April 1994 by the European Parliament stressing the need for new initiatives (see Appendix 4).

This may come about as a result of resolutions on the general situation of the Romanies passed by the Council of Ministers in 1989 and reaffirmed by the Parliament in 1994.

A positive development has been the work of the Centre for Gypsy Research in Paris under the direction of Jean-Pierre Liegeois. Projects funded wholly or partly by the European Union include a newsletter (*Interface*), three working parties (on language, history and education) and support for a series of publications.

By way of a conclusion
As you read these words, over 3,000 families are living on the roadside, on the edge of a sewage farm or perhaps encamped on your local sports field. They have no water supply, rubbish collection and the children are probably not attending school.

The 1968 Caravan Sites Act provided the means by which these families could be given places where they could legally stop while still preserving their independent way of life. Sites are the first step to health and education – and education is one of the means by which Gypsies will become more and more able to stand up for themselves against officialdom and bureaucracy.

The 1968 Act has been repealed and voluntary site provision will never catch up with the birth rate, not unless councillors risk losing votes and permit sites in their area, and the residents, i.e. the general public, become more knowledgeable and able to distinguish the reality about Gypsies from the myths.

All Gypsies, whether on sites or not, suffer from discrimination and harassment. The Race Relations and Public Order Acts should protect them.

We hope that the information in the preceding pages will help to dispel some of the misunderstandings about Gypsies and create a better climate of opinion in which they may integrate, without being assimilated, into the Europe of the twenty first century.

Appendix 1 Addresses

Advisory Council for the Education of Romany and
other Travellers (ACERT)
The Moot House, The Stow, Harlow, Essex CM20 3AG.

British Rommani Union
The Reservation, Hever Road, Edenbridge, Kent TN8 5DJ.

Department of the Environment (Gypsy Sites Branch).
2 Marsham St, London SW1.

East Anglia Gypsy Council
Plot 3, Travellers Site, Oxney Rd, Peterborough, Cambs.

Gypsy Council for Education, Culture, Welfare and Civil
Rights.
8 Hall Road, Aveley, Essex RM15 4HD.

Labour Campaign for Travellers' Rights
1 Westmead Close, Cheshunt, Waltham Cross, Herts E97 6JP.

National Association of Teachers of Travellers
c/o Braybrook Professional Centre, Amos Lane, Wednesfield,
West Midlands WV11 1ND.

National Council for Civil Liberties
21 Tabard St, London SE1.

National Gypsy Council
Greenacres Caravan Site, Hapsford, Helsby, Warrington,
Cheshire WA6 OJS.

Romanestan Publications
22 Northend, Warley, Brentwood, Essex CM14 5LD
(publishers and booksellers)

Romany Guild
The Urban Farm, 50-52 Temple Mills Lane, London E15

National Romani Rights Association
8 Reid Way, King's Lynn, Norfolk PE30 2LL.

Appendix 2 Selective bibliography

ACTON, Thomas. *Gypsy Politics and Social Change*. London: Routledge, Kegan Paul, 1974.

ADAMS, B and others. *Gypsies and Government Policy in England*. London: Heinemann, 1975.

CENTRE FOR GYPSY RESEARCH. *The education of Gypsy and Traveller Children: action research and co-ordination*. Hatfield: University of Hertfordshire Press, 1993.

FORRESTER, Bill. *The Travellers' Handbook*. London: Interchange Books, 1985.

FRASER, A. *The Gypsies*. Oxford: Blackwell, 1992.

KENRICK, Donald. *Gypsies: From India to the Mediterranean*. The Interface Collection. Toulouse: CRDP, 1993.

KENRICK, Donald and PUXON, G. *Destiny of Europe's Gypsies*. London: Heinemann Educational, 1972.

LEBLON, Bernard. *Gypsies and flamenco*. The Interface Collection. Hatfield: University of Hertfordshire Press, 1995.

LIEGEOIS, J-P. *Gypsies*. London: Al-Saaqi, 1986.

LIEGEOIS, J-P. *Roma, Gypsies, Travellers*. Council of Europe, 1995. Forthcoming.

LOWE, R. and SHAW, W. *Travellers, Voices of the New Age Nomads*. London: Fourth Estate, 1993.

MAYALL, David. *English Gypsies and state policies: public power and English Gypsies in the nineteenth and early twentieth century*. The Interface Collection. Hatfield: University of Hertfordshire Press, 1995. Forthcoming.

OKELY, J. *The Traveller-Gypsies*. Cambridge: Cambridge University Press, 1983.

REISS, C. *Education of Gypsy Children*. London: Macmillan, 1975.

RISHI, W.R. *Multilingual Romani Dictionary*. Chandigarh: Roma Publications, 1974.

SANDFORD, J. *Gypsies*. London: Sphere, 1973.

For folk songs see:

KENNEDY, P. *Folksongs of Britain and Ireland*. London: Cassell, 1975.

MacCOLL, E. and SEEGER, P. E. *Travellers' Songs from England and Scotland*. London: Routledge, Kegan Paul, 1977

ROMANO DROM SONG BOOK. Brentwood: Romanestan Publications, 1988.

Topic Records and Folktracks (2 Fircliff Park, Portishead BS10 9HQ) have recorded many Gypsy artists.

Appendix 3 Chronology

1960   *Caravan Sites and Control of Development Act* (controlled private sites).
    Commons Act (stopped camping on commons)

1966   Gypsy Council founded.

1968   *Caravan Sites Act* (see 1970 below)
    Ministry of Housing Circular 49/68 explains the Act.

1970   Part 2 of the *Caravan Sites Act* comes into operation (Councils must provide sites for Gypsies).

1972   First 'designations' under the 1968 Act.

1976   *Race Relations Act* (bans discrimination).

1977   Cripps Report.
    Housing (Homeless Persons) Act (Gypsies with no legal pitch can be counted as homeless).
    Department of the Environment Circular 28/77 (temporary proposals until Cripps Report studied).
    Croydon refuses a school place to a Gypsy on an illegal site.

1978   Circular 57/78 (following up Cripps Report)

1980   Offence of 'being a Gypsy encamping on a highway' abolished.
    Education Act (Gypsies on illegal sites are entitled to a school place).

1981   Brymbo discrimination case.

1985   Rafferty and Gilhaney cases (a county cannot evict

Gypsies without providing an alternative site).

1986   New Age Travellers at Stonehenge.
Statutory Instrument 1986/2289 (reduces to two days the period for giving a trespasser notice to quit).
Public Order Act (Trespass on vacant land becomes a criminal offence; reinforces law on racial harassment)

1987   Wibberley Review (of the 1968 Act)
CRE v. Dutton. First hearing (see below).
Trespass clauses of the *Public Order Act* come into operation.

1988   Greenwich v. Powell, House of Lords.(Confirms Gypsies can be evicted without notice from council sites and defines 'Gypsy').
CRE v. Dutton (Appeal court hearing). No Travellers notices are indirect discrimination.
Education Reform Act. New fund for Traveller education.

1990   4th World Romany Congress, Warsaw.

1994   *Criminal Justice and Public Order Act* (New trespass laws, repeal of 1968 Caravans Site Act).

1   Calls on the governments of the Member States to introduce legal, administrative and social measures to improve the social situation of gypsies and travelling people in Europe;

2   Calls for all citizens of non-member countries legally residing in a Member State, including gypsies, to have the same rights to travel throughout the European Union as citizens of the Union;

3   Recommends that the Governments of the Member States add an additional protocol on minorities to the European Convention of Human Rights, in which the definition of minorities explicitly includes gypsies in the form of a reference to landless minorities;

4   Calls on the Commission and the Council of Europe to draw up a general report on the situation of gypsies in the Member States, with particular regard to coercive measures taken by states, human rights violations, etc.;

5   Recommends that the Commission and Council adopt initiatives in the fields of culture, education, information and equal rights, in the form of proposals to the

governments or the appropriate local and regional authorities of the Member States;

6　Urges that budget items be maintained, and wherever possible increased, in the Community budget for funding such social, cultural and educational action for the gypsy community;

7　Recommends that the Commission, the Council and the governments of the Member States should do everything in their power to assist in the economic, social and political integration of gypsies, with the objective of eliminating the deprivation and poverty in which the great majority of Europe's gypsy population still lives at the present time;

8　Recognises that gypsies are subject to persecution in many countries in central and eastern Europe and therefore recommends the EU Member States should take great care when examining applications for asylum by gypsies from these countries;

9　Condemns the conclusion of repatriation agreements between the Member States of the European Union and the countries of central and eastern Europe which result in refugees being traded like goods;

10　Stresses the need for fresh measures in the educational field, if racism and xenophobia are to be combated effectively, and urges the Commission, the Council and the governments of the Members States to promote a range of measures to help remove the major obstacles to the school education of the children of gypsies and travelling people;

11　Calls on the Commission, the Council and the governments of the Member States to recognise the language and other aspects of gypsy culture as forming an integral part of Europe's cultural heritage;

12 Recommends that the Commission and the Council carry out an in-depth study of the education and training problems facing gypsies and nomads, particularly the schooling of gypsy children who do not have an adequate knowledge of the language of the country or of the region in which they reside; also recommends setting up a specific training programme designed to enable teaching in the gypsy language to be included in curricula, and, as part of its work in the field of inter-cultural education, to prepare information sheets on the subject for teachers;

13 Reminds the Commission, the Council and the governments of the Member States of the decisive role of the media and of local and regional authorities in eliminating racial prejudice and supports full cooperation with the Economic and Social Committee, the Council of Europe and the CSCE to ensure that problems linked to racism and xenophobia are tackled effectively;

14 Urges the Commission and the Member States to implement programmes which provide adequate information for the general public on genuine culture, especially by promoting information programmes carried out by gypsies themselves;

15 Reminds the Community's gypsy citizens of their rights to submit petitions to the European Parliament if they believe themselves to have been the victims of racist behaviour;

16 Calls on the German Government to compensate any gypsies and their families who were victims of Nazi persecution;

17 Calls on the Member States not to expel any gypsies who have fled Romania and the former Yugoslavia and to facilitate the entry of their family members;

18 Urges the Commission and the Council to set up a
European research and information centre, through
which the most representative gypsy organisations could
deal with the Community authorities on all political,
social, or cultural matters involving gypsies;

19 Encourages gypsy organisations to amalgamate at
European level, and calls on the Commission and the
Member States to give financial assistance to such an
amalgamation;

20 Instructs its President to forward this resolution to the
Council, the Commission and the governments of the
Member States.